The All Colour
CHINESE
COOKBOOK

The All Colour
CHINESE
COOKBOOK

Gill Edden

Galley Press

Contents

First published in 1978 by Octopus Books Limited
59 Grosvenor Street, London W1

© 1987 Cathay Books Limited

ISBN 0 86178 489 8

Printed in Hong Kong

Introduction

Forget the mystique that surrounds Chinese cooking and remember the delights of eating a Chinese meal. Put a little thought into selecting a menu and preparing the ingredients and even a beginner can serve a meal full of the flavour and subtlety of the East.

Chinese ingredients
The ingredients used in Chinese cooking are in the main not vastly different from those used in the West.

Left: Onion and ginger crab with egg sauce (page 52)
Below: A selection of ingredients for Chinese cooking

With the exception of a few typically Chinese items, it is the method of cooking and flavouring that make the true distinction. All foods used should be absolutely fresh, or else preserved by drying, pickling or salting; the Chinese are expert at these ancient methods of preserving. Vegetables are often eaten before they mature and always at their peak of freshness. In order that fish may reach the kitchen without a hint of staleness, they are transported inland live, in tanks of water, and are selected while still swimming.

For the less familiar ingredients, listed below, you

7

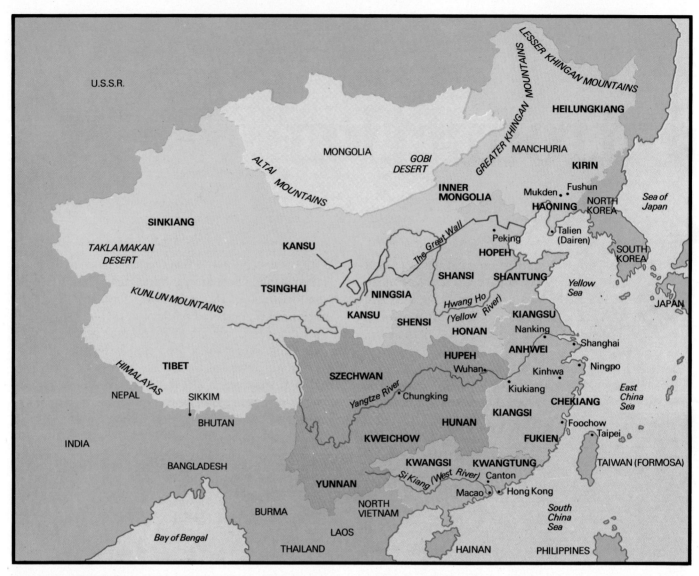

Above: The provinces of China

do not need to trek to the specialist shops found in the Chinese quarters of our large cities (though these shops contain a wealth to fascinate the Westerner). Many good supermarkets and delicatessen stores will stock them and some Chinese restaurants sell the canned and dried foods that are typical of their dishes. Fresh ginger can often be bought at the greengrocer.

Soy sauce is probably the commonest of Chinese flavourings. It is used in all kinds of dishes, but particularly in 'red-cooked' dishes, to which it lends the characteristic colour as well as flavour.

Monosodium glutamate is another common flavouring, a powder that brings out the taste of foods without imparting a flavour of its own. It should be used in moderation, though, as too much can spoil any dish. It is sold under different names, such as Ve-tsin, Ac'cent (in Britain and the US), Zip (in Australia) or just taste or gourmet powder.

Oyster sauce is fairly widely used and many Chinese cooks would make their own, but it is readily available in cans.

Hoisin sauce is a mixture of soya beans and vegetable extracts and is sold canned.

Soy paste is a salty sauce sometimes used to enhance the flavour of a dish.

Soy jam is the sweet version.

Five spice powder is a combination of star anise, anise pepper, fennel, cloves and cinnamon. Use sparingly.

Oils used for cooking are generally vegetable oil or peanut oil, never olive oil which has a pronounced flavour foreign to Chinese cooking.

Ginger appears in many recipes. This is the gnarled, brownish root of the ginger plant; use it fresh if possible as ground ginger can never give the same flavour.

Bamboo shoots are available cooked and ready for use from some Chinese shops, or in cans.

Bean sprouts can be bought canned but should always be rinsed and drained before use. Many Chinese shops sell them fresh, or you can grow your own quite simply using mung beans. These are an important source of vitamins in the Chinese diet.

Black beans are used salted and dried. They are generally available in cans.

Dried mushrooms Chinese dried mushrooms have a flavour quite different from fresh or European dried mushrooms. They must be well soaked in warm water before cooking.

8

Bean curd or bean curd cheese is another soya product. It may be either red or cream coloured.
Snow pickles are salted greens, sold in cans.
Chow chow is preserved fruit, sold in cans.
Waterchestnuts are widely available canned.

Utensils

The true Chinese frying pan is a 'wok'; it has a slightly rounded base and wide sides. Food can be cooked in the base of the pan then pushed to one side to drain while other ingredients are cooking. A good, heavy based conventional frying pan will serve nearly as

Below: Steamed eggs with salt eggs, pickled eggs and quail eggs (page 73)

well, though, and one with a lid is useful as many dishes are simmered as well as fried. Otherwise ordinary saucepans and a heavy casserole are all that is needed.

Most Chinese kitchens would be equipped with a steamer – tiered bamboo baskets in which several dishes can be cooked at a time. An ordinary Western steamer or double boiler will do as well, or you can simply place a heatproof dish or plate in or over a bowl of boiling water.

For most Chinese dishes the food has to be cut into tiny, uniform pieces before cooking. This is traditionally done with a razor sharp chopper but a good cook's knife will serve as well.

9

Above: Chicken chop suey (page 46)
Right: A complete meal, ready to be served

Chinese regional cooking

It is the Cantonese who have been largely responsible for the increase in the number of Chinese restaurants in the West. It is therefore their cooking with which we are most familiar. Many dishes from the Canton region are of the quick stir-fried type. They are not generally highly spiced, though soy sauce is a popular flavouring, and the region is particularly well known for its steamed delicacies such as dumplings, patties and steamed fish, pork and beef.

Fukien has a long sea coast and is famous for its seafood dishes. The region is also said to produce the best soy sauce. Light foods and soups are a speciality here.

Peking is more likely to serve richer foods although plain roasting is also popular. Sweet and sour dishes often have their origins in this region. The Szechwan region also makes good use of a wide range of spices, favouring in particular hot chilli peppers. These are used both in cooking and to serve fresh alongside another dish.

Presenting Chinese food

A Chinese meal will always consist of at least three or four different dishes. These will be served all together with family and guests helping themselves to a little at a time from each dish. For a special occasion six or eight dishes is not unusual. In addition each person will have a bowl of soup, to be drunk throughout the meal, and a dish of rice to eat alternately with the other foods. This way there are no specific 'starter' or 'main' courses and the flavours of every dish blend together.

Sometimes appetizers are served. These would be an assortment of salted nuts or pickles, candied fruits or other small delicacies. These stay on the table throughout the meal.

Ideally the food should be served in china bowls and eaten from china plates and bowls with chopsticks and a china spoon. A hot-plate on the table helps to keep the food warm throughout the duration of the meal.

When selecting a menu, aim to achieve a balance both of ingredients and style of cooking. A menu should include a soup and perhaps a slow-cooked meat dish that can be prepared well in advance, then a variety of quick-cooked dishes, including if possible one with shellfish and one that is largely vegetables. Boiled, steamed or fried rice should always be served. The number of dishes you can serve will depend on the number of guests you are entertaining – it is not usually practical to serve a wide variety of dishes for less than four people.

The recipes in this book do not state how many people they are intended to serve – it all depends how many other dishes are offered.

Rice and noodles

Rice is the most popular bulk food in China and a rice dish of some sort is served with most meals. It may be dry boiled or steamed rice to complement a meat dish with a rich or spicy sauce, or it may be a fried rice dish including other foods such as vegetables or fish. Congee, a rather wet rice dish something like porridge in consistency, is eaten with breakfast, often with a strongly flavoured salt fish.

Noodles are also popular, the most common type being flat, ribbon noodles. Spaghetti can usually be substituted if you don't have Chinese noodles in store, or you can make your own noodles. Home made noodle paste can also be used for hun t'un. Noodles may be served soft or crispy. Soft noodles are simply boiled; crispy noodles (as in a chow mein) are boiled first then fried.

Steamed Rice

Metric/Imperial
100 g/4 oz long grain rice
900 ml–1.2 litres/1½–2 pints salted water

Wash and drain the rice. Cook in boiling salted water for 3 minutes. Drain. Put the rice in a steaming tier and cook for 30 minutes.

American
⅔ cup long grain rice
3¾–5 cups salted water

Boiled Rice

Metric/Imperial
225 g/8 oz long grain rice
450 ml/¾ pint salted water

Wash and drain the rice. Cook in boiling salted water for 5 minutes, stirring occasionally to prevent sticking.

American
1⅓ cups long grain rice
2 cups salted water

Reduce the heat to simmering, cover the pan and cook for 20 minutes or until all the water has been absorbed and the grains are quite separate.

Fried Rice

Metric/Imperial
350 g/12 oz cold cooked rice
salt
pepper
2 × 15 ml spoons/2 tablespoons oil
2 eggs

Season the rice well with salt and pepper. Heat the oil and fry the rice gently over medium heat for about 10 minutes, or until all the oil has been absorbed.

American
2 cups cold cooked rice
salt
pepper
2 tablespoons oil
2 eggs

Beat the eggs until smooth and pour on to the rice in a thin stream, stirring all the time. Heat gently, stirring, until all the egg is evenly distributed and set.

Left: Beef chow mein (page 14)

Beef Chow Mein

Metric/Imperial

350 g/12 oz topside or rump steak
1 × 5 ml spoon/1 teaspoon salt
2 × 5 ml spoons/2 teaspoons sugar
1 × 15 ml spoon/1 tablespoon soy sauce
pinch of monosodium glutamate
4 dried mushrooms
0.5 kg/1 lb bean sprouts
65 g/2½ oz bamboo shoots
4 spring onions
2 × 15 ml spoons/2 tablespoons cornflour
450 ml/¾ pint beef stock
3 × 15 ml spoons/3 tablespoons peanut oil
100 g/4 oz dried egg noodles
oil for deep frying
1 egg

American

¾ lb round or rump steak
1 teaspoon salt
2 teaspoons sugar
1 tablespoon soy sauce
pinch of monosodium glutamate
4 dried mushrooms
8 cups bean sprouts
1 cup bamboo shoots
4 scallions
2 tablespoons cornstarch
2 cups beef stock
3 tablespoons peanut oil
2 cups dried egg noodles
oil for deep frying
1 egg

Cut the beef into strips about 5 mm wide by 5 mm thick and about 5 cm long. Mix together in a bowl the salt, sugar, soy sauce and monosodium glutamate. Marinate the beef in this for 30 minutes.

Soak the mushrooms in warm water for 20 minutes, rinse, squeeze dry and slice, discarding the stalks. Drain the bean sprouts, rinse and drain again. Slice the bamboo shoots into thin strips. Cut the spring onions into 2.5 cm/1 inch lengths. Mix the cornflour and stock together.

Drain the beef and reserve the marinade. Heat the peanut oil and stir fry the beef for 3 to 4 minutes. Add the marinade and cornflour mixture. bring to the boil, stirring constantly, add the vegetables and simmer for 5 minutes.

Cook the noodles in boiling water for 5 minutes; drain thoroughly. Deep fry just before needed and drain well on absorbent kitchen paper. Beat the egg with 1 × 15 ml spoon/1 tablespoon water and pour into a heated, lightly oiled omelet pan. Make a small omelet and cut it into thin strips. Put the noodles on a heated serving dish, top with the beef mixture and garnish with strips of omelet.

Chow Mein with Seafood

Metric/Imperial

350 g/12 oz dried egg noodles
3.5 × 15 ml spoons/3½ tablespoons oil
1 medium onion, sliced
2 rashers bacon, shredded
1 × 225 g/8 oz can clams or crab meat
3 × 15 ml spoons/3 tablespoons soy sauce
2.5 × 15 ml spoons/2½ tablespoons butter
3 slices fresh ginger, shredded
3 cloves garlic, crushed
½ red pepper, shredded
6 oysters
225 g/8 oz prawns or mussels (shelled weight)
3 spring onions, cut into 2.5 cm/1 inch lengths
salt, pepper
1 × 5 ml spoon/1 teaspoon sugar
2 × 15 ml spoons/2 tablespoons dry sherry

American

¾ lb dried egg noodles
3½ tablespoons oil
1 medium onion, sliced
2 slices bacon, shredded
1 × ½ lb can clams or crab meat
3 tablespoons soy sauce
2½ tablespoons butter
3 slices fresh ginger, shredded
3 cloves garlic, crushed
½ red pepper, shredded
6 oysters
½ lb shrimps or mussels (shelled weight)
3 scallions, cut into 1 inch lengths
salt, pepper
1 teaspoon sugar
2 tablespoons dry sherry

Cook the noodles in boiling salted water for 7 to 8 minutes and drain. Rinse in cold water to keep separate. Drain well. Heat oil in a large frying pan over high heat. Add onion and bacon and stir fry for ½ minute. Cook for a further 1 minute. Add clams or crab meat and 2 × 15 ml spoons/ 2 tablespoons of the soy sauce. Stir and turn in the oil for 1 minute. Pour in the cooked noodles and sprinkle with the remaining soy sauce. Stir fry for 1 minute. Reduce the heat to low and simmer gently for 3 to 4 minutes until the noodles are hot through.

Meanwhile, heat the butter in a small frying pan over high heat. When it has melted add the ginger, garlic, red pepper, oysters and prawns. Stir fry for 1 minute. Scatter in the spring onions and add the salt, pepper, sugar and sherry. Stir fry for 1 minute.

Spoon the noodle and clam mixture from the large pan into a large, warmed bowl and spoon the contents of the smaller pan over as a garnish.

Right: Chow mein with seafood

Fried Rice with Ham and Bean Sprouts

Metric/Imperial

2 × 15 ml spoons/2 tablespoons oil
2 spring onions
1 clove garlic, crushed
350 g/12 oz cooked rice
175 g/6 oz cooked ham, chopped
2 × 15 ml spoons/2 tablespoons soy sauce
2 eggs
salt
pepper
225 g/8 oz bean sprouts, drained

American

2 tablespoons oil
2 scallions
1 clove garlic, crushed
2 cups cooked rice
¾ cup chopped, cooked ham
2 tablespoons soy sauce
2 eggs
salt
pepper
½ lb bean sprouts, drained

Heat the oil. Trim and chop the spring onions and fry with the garlic in the oil for 2 minutes over a medium heat. Add the rice, mix well and heat through.

Mix the ham with the soy sauce, add to the rice and mix well. Beat the eggs until smooth, season with salt and pepper. Pour into the rice mixture in a thin stream, stirring all the time, until the eggs are cooked. Stir in the bean sprouts.

Fried Rice with Pork and Shrimps

Metric/Imperial

2 × 15 ml spoons/2 tablespoons oil
2 spring onions
1 clove garlic, crushed
350 g/12 oz cooked rice
175 g/6 oz cooked pork, chopped
100 g/4 oz cooked shrimps
2 × 15 ml spoons/2 tablespoons soy sauce
2 eggs
salt
pepper

American

2 tablespoons oil
2 scallions
1 clove garlic, crushed
2 cups cooked rice
6 oz cooked pork, chopped
½ cup cooked shrimp
2 tablespoons soy sauce
2 eggs
salt
pepper

Heat the oil. Trim and chop the spring onions and fry with the garlic in the oil for 2 minutes over a medium heat. Add the rice, mix well and heat through.

Mix the pork and shrimps with the soy sauce, add to the rice and mix well. Beat the eggs until smooth, season with salt and pepper. Pour into the rice mixture in a thin stream, stirring all the time, until the eggs are cooked.

Noodle Paste

Metric/Imperial
225 g/8 oz plain flour
pinch of salt
1 egg

American
2 cups all-purpose flour
pinch of salt
1 egg

Sift the flour and salt into a mixing bowl. Make a well in the centre and add the egg. Using a round bladed knife, mix the flour into the egg and then add enough water to make a stiff dough. Knead the dough with your hand, very thoroughly. Roll out the dough as thinly as possible on a lightly floured board, lightly flour the surface and roll up the dough like a Swiss roll. Slice it with a sharp knife into 3 mm/⅛ inch slices. Unroll and hang the noodles over a clean cloth over the back of a chair for about 20 minutes, to dry out.
For soft noodles, boil for 5–7 minutes in a large saucepan of boiling salted water.
For crisp noodles, fry in deep hot oil until golden and drain on absorbent kitchen paper. (Noodles made from home made paste do not have to be boiled before frying, as do the dried noodles bought in a shop.)

Below: Fried rice with pork and shrimp(s)

Quick-fried Lamb with Leeks and Rice

Metric/Imperial
0.5 kg/1 lb long grain rice
0.5 kg/1 lb boned leg of lamb
4 × 15 ml spoons/4 tablespoons vegetable oil
1 × 5 ml spoon/1 teaspoon salt
pepper
2 small leeks
2–3 slices fresh ginger, grated
1 × 15 ml spoon/1 tablespoon butter
1½ × 5 ml spoons/1½ teaspoons sugar
2 × 15 ml spoons/2 tablespoons soy sauce
*1 × 15 ml spoon/1 tablespoon cornflour, mixed
    with 4 × 15 ml spoons/4 tablespoons water*
1 × 15 ml spoon/1 tablespoon dry sherry

American
2¼ cups long grain rice
1 lb boned leg of lamb
⅓ cup vegetable oil
1 teaspoon salt
pepper
2 small leeks
2–3 slices fresh ginger, grated
1 tablespoon butter
1½ teaspoons sugar
2 tablespoons soy sauce
*1 tablespoon cornstarch, mixed
    with ⅓ cup water*
1 tablespoon dry sherry

Put the rice in a heavy based saucepan. Rinse once or twice under cold running water, then drain off the water. Add about 550 ml/18 fl oz/2¼ cups fresh water. Bring to the boil, cover with a well fitting lid and place an asbestos sheet under the pan. After 1 minute, reduce the heat to very low and simmer very gently for 10 minutes. Turn the heat off altogether and leave the rice to cook in its own heat for 10 to 12 minutes. Spoon it on to a warmed platter and keep hot.

Slice the lamb thinly, then cut into 2.5 cm/1 inch pieces, mix with a quarter of the oil and sprinkle with salt and pepper. Clean the leeks thoroughly and cut them into 1 cm/½ inch lengths.

Heat the remaining oil in a large frying pan over a high heat. When the oil is very hot add the lamb slices and ginger. Stir and turn a few times, then push them to one side of the pan. Melt the butter in the pan and add the leeks. Stir and turn a few times. Add the sugar and soy sauce and stir fry the lamb and leeks separately for 45 seconds. Pour the cornflour mixture over the lamb and the sherry over the leeks. Mix the two sets of ingredients together for 15 seconds. Spoon the lamb and leek mixture over the hot cooked rice and serve immediately.

Slow-cooked dishes

Slow cooking can make even the cheapest, toughest cut of meat tender. If you bear in mind that all the food on a Chinese table must be capable of being pulled apart with chopsticks you will realise how tender. If you are giving a party with Chinese food you can have one or two slow cooked dishes ready well in advance, for many do not spoil if kept hot in the oven. Some containing chopped meat (as distinct from a whole joint or bird) can even be made the day before, refrigerated and then reheated. Take care when reheating to raise the temperature of the meat sufficiently high to kill off any bacteria; the high temperature must be maintained for at least 15 minutes. If a slow cooked dish is finished with crisp vegetables, or perhaps a slow-simmered chicken is finished by deep frying, complete the slow cooking in advance and leave only the final cooking to be done after the guests have arrived.

Red cooking

Red cooked dishes take their name from the colour of the soy sauce which is the main ingredient. This is a traditional way of stewing meats and apart from the distinctive colour and flavour imparted by the soy, it renders the meat very tender indeed. Pork is the meat most commonly used in red cooked dishes, though any meat or fish can be cooked this way.

Pork and Eggs

Metric/Imperial
1 kg/2 lb lean pork
600 ml/1 pint water
4 × 15 ml spoons/4 tablespoons soy sauce
2 × 15 ml spoons/2 tablespoons dry sherry
1 × 5 ml spoon/1 teaspoon salt
6 eggs
6 spring onions

American
2 lb lean pork
2½ cups water
⅓ cup soy sauce
2 tablespoons dry sherry
1 teaspoon salt
6 eggs
6 scallions

Cut the meat into 2.5 cm/1 inch dice. Put into a pan with the water, bring to the boil, remove the scum, cover and simmer for 30 minutes. Add the soy sauce, sherry and salt. Cook for another 30 minutes.

Boil the eggs for 8 minutes, cool and remove the shells. Make a small slit in the side of each egg and add to the pork. Chop the spring onions, add to the pan and simmer very gently for 5 minutes. Serve very hot.

Left: Pork and eggs

19

Double-cooked Pork

Metric/Imperial

1.5 × 15 ml spoons/1½ tablespoons wood ears
0.75 kg/1½ lb belly pork
2 dried chilli peppers, or 2 × 5 ml spoons/2
   teaspoons chilli sauce
4 spring onions
3.5 × 15 ml spoons/3½ tablespoons vegetable oil
4 cloves garlic, crushed
1 × 15 ml spoon/1 tablespoon soy paste
2 × 15 ml spoons/2 tablespoons soy sauce
1 × 15 ml spoon/1 tablespoon hoisin sauce or
   sweet bean paste
2 × 15 ml spoons/2 tablespoons tomato purée
2 × 5 ml spoons/2 teaspoons sugar
3 × 15 ml spoons/3 tablespoons clear broth (page
   00)
1.5 × 15 ml spoons/1½ tablespoons sherry
1 × 15 ml spoon/1 tablespoon sesame oil

American

1½ tablespoons wood ears
1½ lb belly pork
2 dried chili peppers or 2
   teaspoons chili sauce
4 scallions
3½ tablespoons vegetable oil
4 cloves garlic, crushed
1½ tablespoons soy paste
2 tablespoons soy sauce
1 tablespoon hoisin sauce or sweet
   bean paste
2 tablespoons tomato paste
2 teaspoons sugar
3 tablespoons clear broth
   (page 00)
1½ tablespoons sherry
1 tablespoon sesame oil

Soak the wood ears in water for about 30 minutes. Rinse and drain. Put the pork into a saucepan of boiling water, bring back to the boil and simmer for 25 minutes. Drain and leave to cool. When the pork is cool cut it, through fat and skin, into slices 5 cm × 4 cm/2 inches × 1½ inches.

Cut the chilli peppers into thin slices, discarding the seeds. Trim the spring onions and cut into 4 cm/1½ inch lengths.

Heat the oil in a frying pan over moderate heat. When hot, add the chilli peppers and wood ears and stir fry for 1 minute. Add the garlic, soy paste, soy sauce, hoisin sauce, tomato purée (paste), sugar and broth, stir for 30 seconds, until smooth.

Add the pork pieces to the sauce and spread them out in a single layer. Increase the heat to high and stir and turn the pork in the sauce until it is well coated and the sauce begins to thicken. Sprinkle in the spring onions, sherry and sesame oil. Stir and turn a few more times then turn out on to a warmed dish.

Pork with Chestnuts

Metric/Imperial

1 kg/2 lb lean pork
0.5 kg/1 lb dried skinned chestnuts
4 × 15 ml spoons/4 tablespoons soy sauce
3 × 15 ml spoons/3 tablespoons dry sherry
1 × 5 ml spoon/1 teaspoon brown sugar
0.5 kg/1 lb spinach

American

1 lb lean pork
1 lb dried skinned chestnuts
4 tablespoons soy sauce
3 tablespoons dry sherry
1 teaspoon brown sugar
1 lb spinach

Cut the meat into small cubes. Put into a large pan with 600 ml/1 pint/2½ cups water, bring to the boil, remove the scum, cover with a tightly fitting lid and simmer for 1 hour.

Put the chestnuts into another large pan, cover with cold water, bring to the boil, cover and simmer for 1 hour. Drain the nuts, add to the pork with the soy sauce, sherry and brown sugar. Cook for 20 minutes.

Wash and drain the spinach. Put into a frying pan with 2 × 15 ml spoons/2 tablespoons of the pork liquid. Cook quickly, stirring all the time, for about 5 minutes. Put the spinach into a deep dish, pour pork and liquid over spinach. Serve immediately.

Right: Pork with chestnuts

Sweet and Sour Spare Ribs

Metric/Imperial

1.5 kg/3 lb pork spareribs (American cut)
300 ml/½ pint vinegar
75 g/3 oz cornflour
2 × 15 ml spoons/2 tablespoons honey
1 × 15 ml spoon/1 tablespoon soy sauce
oil for frying
150 ml/¼ pint syrup from canned pineapple
2 × 15 ml spoons/2 tablespoons brown sugar
1 × 2.5 ml spoon/½ teaspoon salt
4 pineapple rings, chopped
1 onion, sliced
1 red pepper, chopped into large pieces

American

3 lb pork spareribs
1¼ cups vinegar
¾ cup cornstarch
2 tablespoons honey
1 tablespoon soy sauce
oil for frying
⅔ cup syrup from canned pineapple
2 tablespoons brown sugar
½ teaspoon salt
4 pineapple rings, chopped
1 onion, sliced
1 red pepper, chopped into large pieces

Cut the spareribs into individual ribs, chopping through the bone if necessary. Half fill a large saucepan with water, add 4 × 15 ml spoons/4 tablespoons of the vinegar and bring to the boil. Add the spareribs and simmer for 20 minutes. Drain.

Put the cornflour, honey and soy sauce in a bowl and mix well. Coat the spareribs with this mixture. Heat about 2.5 cm/1 inch of oil in a large frying pan and fry the spareribs until golden. Drain well on absorbent kitchen paper.

Put the pineapple syrup in a large saucepan with 150 ml/¼ pint/⅔ cup water, the brown sugar, salt and remaining vinegar. Bring to the boil, add the spareribs, cover and simmer for 30 minutes, turning occasionally. Add the pineapple and vegetables to pan 5 minutes before the cooking time is finished.

**Below: Double cooked pork
Right: Sweet and sour spare ribs**

Crispy Pork

Metric/Imperial

0.5 kg/1 lb lean pork
2 × 15 ml spoons/2 tablespoons soy sauce
1 × 15 ml spoon/1 tablespoon sugar
1 clove star anise
1 × 15 ml spoon/1 tablespoon dry sherry
    (optional)
pinch of monosodium glutamate
100 g/4 oz self-raising flour
pinch of salt
1 egg
oil for deep frying

American

1 lb lean pork
2 tablespoons soy sauce
1 tablespoon sugar
1 clove star anise
1 tablespoon dry sherry
    (optional)
pinch of monosodium glutamate
1 cup all-purpose flour
pinch of salt
1 egg
oil for deep frying

Cut the pork into 2.5 cm/1 inch cubes. Put them in a saucepan with 450 ml/¾ pint/2 cups water, soy sauce, sugar, star anise, sherry and monosodium glutamate. Simmer until tender, about 45 minutes. Drain well.

Sift the flour and salt into a bowl. Make a well in the centre, drop in the egg and mix with a wooden spoon, gradually bringing in the flour from around the edge. Gradually beat in 150 ml/¼ pint/½ cup water, beating continually. Add the pork pieces and stir to coat in batter.

Heat the oil and deep fry the coated pork pieces until crisp and golden. Drain well on absorbent kitchen paper. Serve as soon as possible.

Below: Crispy pork

24

Above: Pork and bamboo shoots

Pork and Bamboo Shoots

Metric/Imperial
1 kg/2 lb lean pork
3 × 15 ml spoons/3 tablespoons soy sauce
1 × 15 ml spoon/1 tablespoon dry sherry
1 × 5 ml spoon/1 teaspoon brown sugar
1 × 5 ml spoon/1 teaspoon ground ginger
1.2 litres/2 pints water
100 g/4 oz bamboo shoots
1 × 15 ml spoon/1 tablespoon cornflour (optional)

American
2 lb lean pork
3 tablespoons soy sauce
1 tablespoon dry sherry
1 teaspoon brown sugar
1 teaspoon ground ginger
5 cups water
¼ lb bamboo shoots
*1 tablespoon cornstarch
  (optional)*

Cut the pork into small cubes. Mix the soy sauce, sherry, sugar and ginger together, add to the pork, toss well and leave for 10 minutes.

Put the pork and flavourings into a large pan, add the water and bring gently to the boil. Cover and simmer for 1 hour. Drain the bamboo shoots and

slice finely, add to the pan and simmer for another 10 minutes.

The liquid may be thickened slightly with the cornflour mixed to a smooth paste with a little water, if preferred.

Pork with Mushrooms and Cauliflower

Metric/Imperial
1 kg/2 lb pork chops
100 g/4 oz dried mushrooms
4 × 15 ml spoons/4 tablespoons soy sauce
3 × 15 ml spoons/3 tablespoons dry sherry
4 spring onions
1 × 5 ml spoon/1 teaspoon brown sugar
1 × 5 ml spoon/1 teaspoon salt
1 cauliflower

American
2 lb pork chops
¼ lb dried mushrooms
⅓ cup soy sauce
3 tablespoons dry sherry
4 scallions
1 teaspoon brown sugar
1 teaspoon salt
1 cauliflower

Wipe the chops and put them into a large pan with 600 ml/1 pint/2½ cups water. Bring to the boil, remove the scum, cover the pan with a tight fitting lid and simmer for 30 minutes.

Soak the mushrooms in hot water for 20 minutes, drain and chop finely. Add them to the pan with the soy sauce, sherry, whole spring onions, sugar and salt. Cover and simmer for a further 45 minutes.

Wash the cauliflower and break it into florets. Add to the pan, mix well and cook for a further 15 minutes. Serve immediately.

Pork with Bean Curd

Metric/Imperial
1 kg/2 lb lean pork
4 × 15 ml spoons/4 tablespoons soy sauce
1 × 15 ml spoon/1 tablespoon dry sherry
1 × 5 ml spoon/1 teaspoon brown sugar
1 × 5 ml spoon/1 teaspoon salt
225 g/8 oz bean curd
2 × 15 ml spoons/2 tablespoons oil
1 spring onion

American
2 lb lean pork
⅓ cup soy sauce
1 tablespoon dry sherry
1 teaspoon brown sugar
1 teaspoon salt
½ lb bean curd
2 tablespoons oil
1 scallion

Cut the pork into small dice and put into a pan with 600 ml/1 pint/2½ cups water. Bring to the boil, remove the scum, cover the pan and simmer for 1 hour. Add 2 × 15 ml spoons/2 tablespoons of the soy sauce, all the sherry, sugar and salt. Cover and cook for another 30 minutes.

Cut the bean curd into pieces 5 cm/2 inches square. Heat the oil and fry the bean curd for 2 to 3 minutes, turning it over once during cooking. Add the remaining soy sauce, 300 ml/½ pint/1¼ cups water and the spring onion, cut into small pieces. Stir well and cook for 10 minutes, stirring occasionally. Mix the bean curd mixture into the pork and pour into a dish. Serve immediately.

Barbecued Pork with Bean Sprouts

Metric/Imperial

0.5 kg/1 lb lean pork
1 spring onion
2 slices fresh ginger
4 × 15 ml spoons/4 tablespoons hoisin or soy sauce
2 × 15 ml spoons/2 tablespoons dry sherry
1 clove garlic, crushed
2 × 15 ml spoons/2 tablespoons honey
1 × 15 ml spoon/1 tablespoon peanut oil
1 × 5 ml spoon/1 teaspoon very finely chopped
  fresh ginger
1 × 2.5 ml spoon/½ teaspoon salt
0.5 kg/1 lb bean sprouts
1 × 5 ml spoon/1 teaspoon sugar

American

1 lb lean pork
1 scallion
2 slices fresh ginger
⅓ cup hoisin or soy sauce
2 tablespoons dry sherry
1 clove garlic, crushed
2 tablespoons honey
1 tablespoon peanut oil
1 teaspoon very finely chopped
  fresh ginger
½ teaspoon salt
1 lb bean sprouts
1 teaspoon sugar

Cut the pork into strips 5 cm × 2.5 cm × 2.5 cm/2 inches × 1 inch × 1 inch. Chop the spring onion finely and mix it with the ginger, hoisin sauce, sherry and garlic. Add the pork strips, coat with the marinade and leave for 4 to 6 hours, stirring occasionally.

Drain the pork and mix with honey. Place it on a greased rack in a roasting pan containing 2.5 cm/1 inch of water. Cook at 180°C/350°F/Gas Mark 4 for 25 minutes. Slice into thin pieces.

Heat the oil in a saucepan. Add the chopped ginger and salt and fry for 2 minutes. Drain the bean sprouts, rinse in cold running water, drain again and add to the saucepan with 1 tablespoon 1 × 15 ml spoon/water and the sugar. Heat gently, stirring until well mixed. Add the pork, cover and heat through.

Left: Pork with bean curd
**Below: Pork with mushrooms
and cauliflower**

Red-cooked Fish with Onions and Spring Onions (Scallions)

Metric/Imperial

0.75 kg/1½ lb fish, such as cod, haddock, turbot, carp, rock salmon
1 × 15 ml spoon/1 tablespoon flour
1 × 5 ml spoon/1 teaspoon salt
2–3 slices fresh ginger, grated
3.5 × 15 ml spoons/3½ tablespoons soy sauce
3 × 15 ml spoons/3 tablespoons red wine or sherry
1½ × 5 ml spoons/1½ teaspoons sugar
5 × 15 ml spoons/5 tablespoons oil
2 onions, sliced thinly
3 spring onions

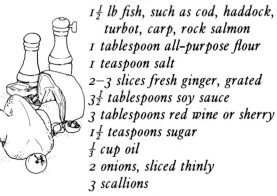

American

1½ lb fish, such as cod, haddock, turbot, carp, rock salmon
1 tablespoon all-purpose flour
1 teaspoon salt
2–3 slices fresh ginger, grated
3½ tablespoons soy sauce
3 tablespoons red wine or sherry
1½ teaspoons sugar
⅓ cup oil
2 onions, sliced thinly
3 scallions

Cut the fish into 4 cm/1½ inch pieces. Mix them with the flour, salt and ginger. Leave for 30 minutes. Mix the soy sauce, wine or sherry and sugar until they are well blended.

Heat 2 × 15 ml spoons/2 tablespoons of the oil in a frying pan over moderate heat. Add the onions and stir fry for 2 minutes. Push them to one side of the pan. Add the remaining oil. When it is hot add the fish pieces and fry for 2 minutes on each side. Pour in the soy sauce mixture and toss the fish pieces in it until they are well coated. Mix the onions into the sauce, then spoon them over the fish. Cut the spring onions into 2.5 cm/1 inch lengths and sprinkle over the onions. cover the pan and cook for 3 to 4 minutes.

Serve on a warmed platter, on a bed of boiled rice.

Stewed Lamb with Orange

Metric/Imperial

1 kg/2 lb lean lamb
1 × 15 ml spoon/1 tablespoon soy sauce
1 × 15 ml spoon/1 tablespoon dry sherry
1 × 5 ml spoon/1 teaspoon ground ginger
2 × 15 ml spoons/2 tablespoons finely grated orange rind
1 × 5 ml spoon/1 teaspoon salt
1.2 litres/2 pints stock or water
1 × 15 ml/1 tablespoon cornflour

American

2 lb lean lamb
1 tablespoon soy sauce
1 tablespoon dry sherry
1 teaspoon ground ginger
2 tablespoons finely grated orange rind
1 teaspoon salt
5 cups stock or water
1 tablespoon cornstarch

Cut the meat into 1 cm/½ inch dice. Mix the soy sauce, sherry, ginger, orange rind and salt together, add to the lamb and mix well. Put the lamb into a pan with the flavourings and stock or water. Bring to the boil, remove the scum, cover and simmer for 2 hours. Mix the cornflour to a smooth paste with a little cold water and add to the pan. Bring back to the boil, stirring until slightly thickened.

Jellied Lamb

Metric/Imperial

1.5 kg/3 lb leg of lamb
4 spring onions, chopped
1 × 5 ml spoon/1 teaspoon salt
4 × 15 ml spoons/4 tablespoons soy sauce

American

3 lb leg of lamb
4 scallions, chopped
1 teaspoon salt
⅓ cup soy sauce

Cut the lamb into small pieces and chop the bones small. Put the spring onions in a large saucepan with the lamb, bones and salt. Cover with cold water and bring to the boil. Remove the scum, add the soy sauce, cover the pan and simmer for 2½ hours. Remove all the bones and pick the meat into small pieces. Put it into a straight sided dish with some of the cooking liquid and press down with a weight on top. Leave until cold and set. Cut into slices to serve.

Right: Red cooked fish with onions and spring onions (scallions)

Above: Spiced leg or shoulder of lamb

Spiced Whole Lamb

Metric/Imperial

1.5 kg/3 lb leg or shoulder of lamb
1 × 5 ml spoon/1 teaspoon salt
1 × 15 ml spoon/1 tablespoon soy sauce
1 × 15 ml spoon/1 tablespoon dry sherry
2 cloves garlic, crushed
25 g/1 oz fresh ginger, shredded or 1 × 5 ml
   spoon/1 teaspoon ground ginger
4 × 15 ml spoons/4 tablespoons oil
1.2 litres/2 pints stock
1 × 15 ml spoon/1 tablespoon cornflour

American

3 lb leg or shoulder of lamb
1 teaspoon salt
1 tablespoon soy sauce
1 tablespoon dry sherry
2 cloves garlic, crushed
1 tablespoon fresh ginger,
   shredded or 1 teaspoon ground
   ginger
⅓ cup oil
5 cups stock
1 tablespoon cornstarch

Wipe the meat and rub the salt into the skin. Put it into a pan with enough cold water to cover, bring to the boil, remove the scum, cover and simmer for 20 minutes. Drain off the liquid. Mix the soy sauce, sherry, garlic and ginger and rub into the lamb. Leave for 10 minutes.

Heat the oil and fry the lamb for about 15 minutes, turning it to brown all over. Add the

stock, bring to the boil, cover and simmer for 2½ hours.

Mix the cornflour to a smooth paste with a little cold water. Lift the lamb on to a hot dish and keep it hot. Add the cornflour to the liquid in the pan and bring to the boil, stirring all the time until slightly thickened. Pour the sauce over the lamb.

Simmering

Simmering is long slow cooking in clear broth or water. It is similar to the method used for our own boiled beef or boiled chicken, but flavouring vegetables are not included in the broth; these are added only in the final stages of cooking. After simmering, the meat is often pulled apart for final dressing and serving.

Braising uses rather less liquid and includes more flavourings right from the start. The cooking liquid is then generally used in a sauce with the finished dish. The length of the cooking time is still important as the meat must be chopstick tender when served.

Slow-simmered Chicken

Metric/Imperial
$1\frac{1}{2}$–2 kg/3–4 lb chicken
2 × 5 ml spoons/2 teaspoons salt
3–4 slices fresh ginger, peeled and chopped
1 chicken stock cube
2 onions, quartered
3 × 15 ml spoons/3 tablespoons snow pickles, or gherkins
1 Chinese or Savoy cabbage, cut into wedges

American
3–4 lb chicken
2 teaspoons salt
3–4 slices fresh ginger, peeled and chopped
1 chicken bouillon cube
2 onions, quartered
3 tablespoons snow pickles, or gherkins
1 Chinese or Savoy cabbage, cut into wedges

Blanch the chicken in boiling water for 6 minutes, skimming any scum from the surface. Drain well. Rub it inside and out with the salt and stuff with a mixture of the ginger, crumbled stock cube, onion and pickles.

Put the stuffed chicken in a flameproof casserole with 1.2 litres/2 pints/5 cups water. Bring to the boil and put the casserole into the oven, preheated to 180°C/350°F/Gas Mark 4. Cook for 1 hour 20 minutes, turning the chicken once. Then take the chicken out of the casserole, arrange the cabbage wedges in the liquid and replace the chicken on top. Return the casserole to the oven and cook for a further 40 minutes.

Serve straight from the casserole or transfer to a very large warmed bowl or tureen.

Chicken with Celery and Pineapple Sauce

Metric/Imperial
1.25 kg/$2\frac{1}{2}$ lb chicken
2 sticks celery
3 pineapple rings
1 × 15 ml spoon/1 tablespoon cornflour
1 × 15 ml spoon/1 tablespoon soy sauce
1 × 2.5 ml spoon/$\frac{1}{2}$ teaspoon very finely chopped fresh ginger
4 × 15 ml spoons/4 tablespoons syrup from canned pineapple
4 × 15 ml spoons/4 tablespoons brown sugar
4 × 15 ml spoons/4 tablespoons vinegar
salt
pepper
1 egg
extra cornflour
oil for deep frying

American
$2\frac{1}{4}$ lb chicken
2 stalks celery
3 pineapple rings
1 tablespoon cornstarch
1 tablespoon soy sauce
$\frac{1}{2}$ teaspoon very finely chopped fresh ginger
$\frac{1}{3}$ cup syrup from canned pineapple
$\frac{1}{3}$ cup brown sugar
$\frac{1}{3}$ cup vinegar
salt
pepper
1 egg
extra cornstarch
oil for deep frying

Place the chicken in a large saucepan and cover with water. Bring to the boil then simmer until tender. This will be about 1 hour for a young bird or 2–3 hours for a boiling fowl. Drain and allow to cool.

Cut the celery into diagonal slices and the pineapple rings into wedges. In a saucepan, mix together the cornflour, soy sauce and ginger with 4 × 15 ml spoons/4 tablespoons/$\frac{1}{3}$ cup water and the pineapple syrup and sugar. Bring to the boil, stirring constantly, stir in the vinegar and cook for 2 minutes. Remove from the heat and add the celery and pineapple wedges. Season to taste.

Cut the cooled chicken into quarters, cut each quarter in half to make 8 pieces. Beat the egg with a little salt and pepper. Dip the chicken pieces in egg and then in cornflour. Shake off the excess cornflour and deep fry the chicken in hot oil until golden.

Arrange the chicken on a serving dish. Reheat the sauce and pour it over the chicken pieces.

Braised Chicken with Peppers

Metric/Imperial

1 kg/2 lb chicken
3 sweet peppers
3 × 15 ml spoons/3 tablespoons oil
1 × 5 ml spoon/1 teaspoon salt
25 g/1 oz fresh ginger
pinch of brown sugar
2 × 5 ml spoons/2 teaspoons dry sherry
1 × 5 ml spoon/1 teaspoon cornflour
2 × 5 ml spoons/2 teaspoons soy sauce

American

2 lb chicken
3 sweet peppers
3 tablespoons oil
1 teaspoon salt
1 tablespoon fresh ginger
pinch of brown sugar
2 teaspoons dry sherry
1 teaspoon cornstarch
2 teaspoons soy sauce

Put the chicken in a large saucepan and cover with water. Bring to the boil then simmer until tender. Drain and allow to cool. When the chicken is cool, remove the meat from the bones and cut into 2.5 cm/1 inch pieces; there should be about 0.5 kg/1 lb meat.

Deseed peppers and cut into thin rings. Heat 1 × 15 ml spoon/1 tablespoon oil in a large frying pan, add the peppers and salt and fry for 1 minute. Add 2 × 15 ml spoons/2 tablespoons water, bring to the boil, cover and simmer for 2 minutes. Drain.

Chop the ginger finely. Fry the chicken and ginger in the remaining oil for 1 minute. Add the sugar and sherry.

Mix the cornflour to a smooth paste with the soy sauce and add to the pan. Heat gently, stirring until slightly thickened. Add the peppers and cook for 1 minute more, then serve immediately.

Sweet and Sour Chicken Salad

Metric/Imperial

1.25 kg/2½ lb chicken
1 × 5 ml spoon/1 teaspoon dry mustard
1 × 2.5 ml spoon/½ teaspoon salt
1 × 2.5 ml spoon/½ teaspoon ground black pepper
4 × 15 ml spoons/4 tablespoons white wine vinegar
6 × 15 ml spoons/6 tablespoons peanut oil
2 cloves garlic, crushed
1 × 5 ml spoon/1 teaspoon soy sauce
1 × 15 ml spoon/1 tablespoon honey
about 8 snow pickles or small gherkins, sliced
4 rings pineapple, diced
1 × 15 ml spoon/1 tablespoon raisins
2 × 15 ml spoons/2 tablespoons blanched flaked almonds
endive or lettuce

American

2½ lb chicken
1 teaspoon dry mustard
½ teaspoon salt
¼ teaspoon ground black pepper
⅓ cup white wine vinegar
6 tablespoons peanut oil
2 cloves garlic, crushed
1 teaspoon soy sauce
1 tablespoon honey
about 8 snow pickles, or small dill pickles, sliced
4 rings pineapple, diced
1 tablespoon raisins
2 tablespoons blanched flaked almonds
chicory or lettuce

Put the chicken in a large saucepan and cover with water. Bring to the boil then simmer until tender. Drain and allow to cool then cut the chicken into small, neat pieces.

Blend the mustard, salt and pepper with the vinegar then add the oil, garlic, soy sauce and honey. Stir in the sliced pickles, pineapple and raisins. Mix in the pieces of chicken and leave to stand for 15 minutes. If the chicken has not absorbed all the marinade, spoon this out of the bowl and sprinkle over the salad at the last minute.

Wash the endive (chicory) or lettuce and arrange on a large serving dish. Mix the nuts into the chicken and spoon the salad into the centre of the endive (chicory).

Right: Sweet and sour chicken salad

Golden Braised Fish

Metric/Imperial

1 kg/2 lb whole fish (eg. bream or bass)
salt
plain flour
4 dried mushrooms
4 spring onions
6 water chestnuts
oil for frying
1 × 5 ml spoon/1 teaspoon very finely chopped
  fresh ginger
300 ml/½ pint fish stock or water
2 × 15 ml spoons/2 tablespoons soy sauce
1 × 15 ml spoon/1 tablespoon sherry
1 × 5 ml spoon/1 teaspoon salt
2 cloves garlic, crushed
1 clove star anise
1 × 5 ml spoon/1 teaspoon sugar

American

2 lb whole fish (eg. bass or
  snapper)
salt
all-purpose flour
4 dried mushrooms
4 scallions
6 water chestnuts
oil for frying
1 teaspoon very finely chopped
  fresh ginger
1¼ cups fish stock or water
2 tablespoons soy sauce
1 tablespoon sherry
1 teaspoon salt
2 cloves garlic, crushed
1 clove star anise
1 teaspoon sugar

Clean the fish, leaving on the head and tail. Wipe inside and out with kitchen paper. Make two gashes on each side, in the thickest part. Sprinkle with salt and coat in flour. Soak the mushrooms in warm water for 20 minutes, rinse, squeeze dry and discard the stalks. Cut the mushrooms into strips and the spring onions into 1 cm/½ inch lengths. Slice the water chestnuts.

Heat a little oil in a large frying pan and when hot, fry the fish on both sides until golden. Pour off the excess oil and add the rest of the ingredients. Cover the pan, bring to the boil and simmer for about 30 minutes, turning the fish once. Serve on a large heated plate with the sauce poured over.

Crisp Skin Chicken

Metric/Imperial

1.25 kg/2½ lb chicken
1 × 15 ml spoon/1 tablespoon vinegar
2 × 15 ml spoons/2 tablespoons soy sauce
2 × 15 ml spoons/2 tablespoons honey
1 × 15 ml spoon/1 tablespoon dry sherry
1 × 5 ml spoon/1 teaspoon golden syrup
2 × 15 ml spoons/2 tablespoons plain flour
1 × 5 ml spoon/1 teaspoon salt
oil for deep frying

American

2½ lb chicken
1 tablespoon vinegar
2 tablespoons soy sauce
2 tablespoons honey
1 tablespoon dry sherry
1 teaspoon light corn syrup
2 tablespoons all-purpose flour
1 teaspoon salt
oil for deep frying

Put the chicken in a large saucepan and add boiling water to come halfway up the sides of the chicken. Cover tightly and simmer until just tender, about 45 minutes to 1 hour. Drain, rinse under cold water and dry with absorbent kitchen paper.

Mix together the vinegar, soy sauce, honey, sherry and syrup. Brush this all over the chicken and then hang the chicken in an airy place to dry for about 30 minutes. Brush over again with the remaining soy sauce mixture and hang again for 20 to 30 minutes.

Mix the flour and salt together and rub well into the chicken skin. Fry in deep oil until golden and crisp. Drain well on absorbent kitchen paper. Chop the chicken into 8 pieces and serve warm with dips.

Cinnamon dip

Mix together 1 × 15 ml spoon/1 tablespoon ground cinnamon, 1 × 2.5 ml spoon/½ teaspoon ground ginger, ½ × 2.5 ml spoon/¼ teaspoon each freshly ground black pepper and salt. Put in a small saucepan, heat until very hot, stirring constantly.

Pepper and salt dip

Mix together 1 × 15 ml spoon/1 tablespoon salt and ½ × 15 ml spoon/½ tablespoon freshly ground black pepper. Put in a small saucepan and heat, stirring, until the salt begins to brown.

Serve the dips separately in small bowls, alongside a bowl of hoisin sauce (served cold). Guests eat the chicken with their fingers, dipping each piece into the dips and sauce. Place finger bowls of cold water on the table.

Right: Crisp skin chicken

Sweet Chicken Wings with Oyster Sauce

Metric/Imperial

0.5 kg/1 lb chicken wings
3 × 15 ml spoons/3 tablespoons canned oyster
  sauce
1 × 15 ml spoon/1 tablespoon soy sauce
300 ml/½ pint chicken stock
pinch of salt
1 × 5 ml spoon/1 teaspoon brown sugar
25 g/1 oz fresh ginger
pinch of black pepper
1 × 5 ml spoon/1 teaspoon coarse salt

American

1 lb chicken wings
3 tablespoons canned oyster sauce
1 tablespoon soy sauce
1¼ cups chicken stock
pinch of salt
1 teaspoon brown sugar
1 oz fresh ginger
pinch of black pepper
1 teaspoon coarse salt

Wash and dry the chicken wings. Put them in a pan with enough cold water to cover, bring to the boil, cover and simmer for 10 minutes. Drain.

Put the chicken wings into a clean pan and add the oyster sauce, soy sauce, chicken stock, salt and sugar. Bring gently to the boil and simmer for 20 minutes.

Chop the ginger very finely and add to it the black pepper and coarse salt. Sprinkle over the chicken and serve.

Onion and Leek Wine-simmered Duck

Metric/Imperial

6 medium dried mushrooms
2 kg/4–4½ lb duck
4 slices fresh ginger
2 small leeks
4 medium onions
5 × 15 ml spoons/5 tablespoons vegetable oil
1 × 5 ml spoon/1 teaspoon salt
4 × 15 ml spoons/4 tablespoons soy sauce
300 ml/½ pint red wine
1 chicken stock cube

American

6 medium dried mushrooms
4–4½ lb duck
4 slices fresh ginger
2 small leeks
4 medium onions
⅓ cup vegetable oil
1 teaspoon salt
⅓ cup soy sauce
1¼ cups red wine
1 chicken bouillon cube

Soak the dried mushrooms in 300 ml/½ pint/1¼ cups water for 30 minutes. Reserve the soaking water. Remove the stalks and cut the caps into quarters. Clean the duck under cold running water. Trim off any excess fat. Peel and chop the ginger. Clean the leeks thoroughly and cut into 5 cm/2 inch lengths. Cut the onions in half.

Fry the onions in the oil for 4 to 5 minutes and drain. Fry the duck in the same oil for 5 to 6 minutes until lightly browned. Stuff the cavity of the duck with the ginger, onions, salt and mushrooms.

Put the duck in a heavy based saucepan or flameproof casserole. Add half the soy sauce and 900 ml/1½ pints/3¾ cups water. Bring to the boil, cover and simmer gently for 45 minutes, turning it over once. Leave to cool. When the cooking liquid is cold, skim off any scum from the surface and discard two-thirds of the liquid. Add the wine, the reserved mushroom soaking water, the remaining soy sauce and the crumbled stock cube. Bring to the boil. Simmer very gently for 1 hour or until the liquid is reduced by half, turning the duck over twice.

Remove the duck from the pan and put in a warmed, deep-sided dish to keep hot. Add the leeks to the cooking pan, increase the heat to high and boil rapidly until the liquid is reduced by half. Spoon the sauce from the pan over the duck and arrange the leeks round it.

Right: Onion and leek wine-simmered duck

Braised Duck with Sweet and Pungent Sauce

Metric/Imperial

1.75 kg/4 lb duck
salt
1 clove garlic, crushed
3 spring onions, very finely chopped
3 × 15 ml spoons/3 tablespoons soy sauce
2 × 15 ml spoons/2 tablespoons sherry
2 × 15 ml spoons/2 tablespoons honey
SAUCE:
1 small green pepper
150 g/5 oz bamboo shoots
2 dried mushrooms
2 × 15 ml spoons/2 tablespoons oil
1 × 5 ml spoon/1 teaspoon finely chopped fresh
   ginger
1 clove garlic, crushed
150 ml/¼ pint stock
2 × 15 ml spoons/2 tablespoons honey
150 ml/¼ pint pineapple juice
2 × 15 ml spoons/2 tablespoons vinegar
1 × 5 ml spoon/1 teaspoon tomato purée
1 × 15 ml spoon/1 tablespoon dry sherry
1 × 15 ml spoon/1 tablespoon soy sauce
salt
pepper
2 × 15 ml spoons/2 tablespoons cornflour
GARNISH:
340 g/11 oz can mandarin oranges
4 pineapple rings, chopped

American

4 lb duck
salt
1 clove garlic, crushed
3 scallions, very finely chopped
3 tablespoons soy sauce
2 tablespoons sherry
2 tablespoons honey
SAUCE:
1 small green pepper
5 oz bamboo shoots
2 dried mushrooms
2 tablespoons oil
1 teaspoon finely chopped fresh
   ginger
1 clove garlic, crushed
⅔ cup stock
2 tablespoons honey
⅔ cup pineapple juice
2 tablespoons vinegar
1 teaspoon tomato paste
1 tablespoon dry sherry
1 tablespoon soy sauce
salt
pepper
2 tablespoons cornstarch
GARNISH:
11 oz can mandarin oranges
4 pineapple rings, chopped

Wipe the duck inside and out with a damp cloth and rub it all over with salt. Mix the garlic, spring onions, soy sauce and sherry together. Divide the mixture into two and mix the honey into one half. Rub the outside of the duck with some of the honey mixture and leave to dry.

Put the duck on a rack in a roasting pan and pour the soy sauce mixture (*not* the honey mixture) inside. Pour 5 cm/2 inches of water into the roasting pan and cook the duck in a preheated moderate oven (180°C/350°F/Gas Mark 4) for 1¾ to 2 hours or until tender, with the flesh coming away from the bones easily. Add 300 ml/½ pint/1¼ cups boiling water to the remaining honey mixture and baste with this every 20 minutes during cooking.

Cut the pepper into wedges and the bamboo shoots into thin strips. Soak the mushrooms in warm water for 20 minutes, rinse, squeeze dry and slice, discarding the stalks.

Put the oil in a saucepan and fry the prepared vegetables with the ginger and garlic for 5 minutes. Add the stock and bring to the boil. Add the honey, pineapple juice and vinegar, bring to the boil again and stir until the honey has melted. Stir in tomato purée (paste), sherry, soy sauce and season with salt and pepper to taste. Mix the cornflour with a little water and add to the sauce in the pan. Bring to the boil stirring constantly and simmer for 2 to 3 minutes.

Put the duck on a large serving dish and garnish with the mandarin oranges and pineapple. Pour the sauce over and serve hot.

Note: Make the stock from the duck giblets or use a chicken stock cube.

Right: Braised duck with sweet and pungent sauce

Steaming

Steaming demands the highest quality food but if done slowly is ideal for a thick slice of meat or a whole fish. It involves careful cooking over a steady, even heat. Traditionally a Chinese steamer consists of tiers of bamboo baskets with the water pot at the bottom and the steam percolating through the basketwork. An ordinary double boiler gives much the same effect.

Crab with Black Beans

Metric/Imperial

2 × 200 g/7 oz cans crab meat
25 g/1 oz black beans
1 clove garlic, crushed
2 × 5 ml spoons/2 teaspoons sherry
2 × 5 ml spoons/2 teaspoons oil
pinch ground ginger

American

2 × 7 oz cans crab meat
½ cup black beans
1 clove garlic, crushed
2 teaspoons sherry
2 teaspoons oil
pinch ground ginger

Drain the crab and chop the meat finely. Arrange it in the base of a greased shallow dish. Put the beans in boiling water, bring them back to the boil, then drain and cool under cold running water. Mash them with a fork. Mix in the garlic, sherry, oil and ginger. Beat well to make a smooth paste.

Spread the bean mixture over the crab. Cover the dish and steam gently for 45 minutes. Serve directly from the bowl in which it was cooked.

Below: Crab with black beans

Above: Ham with lotus seeds in honey sauce

Ham with Lotus Seeds in Honey Sauce

Metric/Imperial

1 × 5 cm/2 inch thick slice ham (about 1–1.25
  kg/2–2½ lb)
3 × 15 ml spoons/3 tablespoons brown sugar
0.5 × 2.5 ml spoon/¼ teaspoon ground cinnamon
6 × 15 ml spoons/6 tablespoons water
300 ml/½ pint lotus seeds or peanuts
HONEY SAUCE:
3 × 15 ml spoons/3 tablespoons clear honey
1.5 × 15 ml spoons/1½ tablespoons sugar
2 × 5 ml spoons/2 teaspoons cornflour, mixed with
3 × 15 ml spoons/3 tablespoons water

American

1 × 2 inch thick slice ham (about
  2–2½ lb)
3 tablespoons brown sugar
¼ teaspoon ground cinnamon
6 tablespoons water
1½ cups lotus seeds or peanuts
HONEY SAUCE:
3 tablespoons clear honey
1¼ tablespoons sugar
2 teaspoons cornstarch, mixed
  with 3 tablespoons water

Put the ham, in one piece, on a heatproof dish. Put into a steamer and steam steadily for 1 hour. Cut the ham into pieces and return them to the dish.

Put the brown sugar, cinnamon and water into a small saucepan and heat until the sugar has dissolved. Add the lotus seeds or peanuts and stir and turn in the syrup for 2 minutes then spoon over the ham. Return the dish to the steamer and steam steadily for a further 1½ hours.

Combine all the sauce ingredients in a small saucepan until they are well blended then heat gently, stirring constantly, until slightly thickened. Pour over the lotus seeds and ham.

Quick-cooked dishes

Quick cooking produces much of the food that to Western eyes is most typically Chinese. Quick cooking includes frying, roasting and steaming, but in all cases requires top quality ingredients to achieve a tender, succulent dish. Every Chinese meal will include one or two of these dishes, prepared at the last moment when the family and guests are almost ready to sit down. They are also popular in restaurants as all the preparation can be done well in advance and the meal can be served quickly once ordered.

Stir frying

Stir frying is a process of cooking in a little fat or oil at a high heat, to seal in the natural juices of the food and cook it through quickly. For stir fried dishes all the ingredients must be cut into fine strips of even size or into thin slices. They will then cook through in the minimum of time and give the most tasty, tender result.

Fine cuts of meat such as pork fillet (tenderloin) and beef fillet are essential, but a stir fried dish usually includes a variety of vegetables as well, so a little meat goes a long way. Shellfish are popular in stir fried dishes as they are ideally suited to quick cooking.

Ingredients are generally added one at a time and cooked quickly, stirring all the time to ensure even cooking. When the first ingredient is cooked it is pushed to one side of the pan and the oil reheated before the next ingredient is added. When all the ingredients are cooked they are mixed together for the final cooking to reheat and blend the flavours. After frying, a small amount of liquid is often added to make an integral sauce.

Pork with Bean Sprouts and Almonds

Metric/Imperial
350 g/12 oz shoulder or spring of pork
0.5 kg/1 lb bean sprouts
50 g/2 oz blanched almonds
1 × 15 ml spoon/1 tablespoon soy sauce
2 × 15 ml spoons/2 tablespoons chicken stock
1 × 5 ml spoon/1 teaspoon sugar
2 × 15 ml spoons/2 tablespoons peanut oil
2 spring onions, thinly sliced
1 pineapple ring, chopped
salt
pepper

American
¾ lb picnic shoulder pork
1 lb bean sprouts
½ cup blanched almonds
1 tablespoon soy sauce
2 tablespoons chicken stock
1 teaspoon sugar
2 tablespoons peanut oil
2 scallions, thinly sliced
1 pineapple ring, chopped
salt
pepper

Cut the pork into 1 cm/½ inch cubes. Drain the bean sprouts, rinse in cold running water and drain again. Halve the almonds. Mix together the soy sauce, stock and sugar.

Heat the oil in a frying pan and fry the pork, stirring, until it changes colour. Add the almonds and spring onions and fry for 3 to 4 minutes. Pour off any oil. Add all the other ingredients, including the bean sprouts. Combine thoroughly, cover the pan and cook for 2 minutes.

Left: Pork with bean sprouts and almonds

Lamb and Vermicelli

Metric/Imperial

100 g/4 oz Chinese vermicelli
225 g/8 oz lean lamb meat
1 × 5 ml spoon/1 teaspoon cornflour
1 egg
1 × 15 ml spoon/1 tablespoon oil
2 × 5 ml spoons/2 teaspoons soy sauce
2 × 15 ml spoons/2 tablespoons tomato ketchup
1 × 15 ml spoon/1 tablespoon sherry
pinch of salt
pinch of black pepper
3 spring onions
300 ml/½ pint stock

American

¼ lb Chinese bean threads
½ lb lean lamb meat
1 teaspoon cornstarch
1 egg
1 tablespoon oil
2 teaspoons soy sauce
2 tablespoons tomato catsup
1 tablespoon sherry
pinch of salt
pinch of black pepper
3 scallions
1¼ cups stock

Soak the vermicelli in hot water for 10 minutes. Cut the meat into strips about 4 cm long by 5 mm wide (1½ inches × ¼ inch). Mix the cornflour to a smooth paste with 1 × 15 ml spoon/1 tablespoon water, add the egg and beat well. Add to the lamb and toss to coat the meat completely.

Heat the oil and fry the meat quickly, stirring all the time, for 2 to 3 minutes. Drain. Add the vermicelli to the pan, stir well and cook for 2 to 3 minutes. Mix the soy sauce, tomato ketchup, sherry, salt and pepper together and add to the vermicelli with the meat. Mix well. Chop the spring onions finely, add to the pan, and cook for 1 minute. Add the stock, bring to the boil and cook for 5 minutes. Serve immediately.

Kidney with Spring Onions (Scallions) and Cauliflower

Metric/Imperial

4 lamb kidneys
2 × 15 ml spoons/2 tablespoons sherry
1 small cauliflower
4 spring onions
2 × 15 ml spoons/2 tablespoons oil or melted lard
1 × 15 ml spoon/1 tablespoon cornflour
1 × 15 ml spoon/1 tablespoon soy sauce
1 × 5 ml spoon/1 teaspoon brown sugar
1 × 5 ml spoon/1 teaspoon salt

American

4 lamb kidneys
2 tablespoons sherry
1 small cauliflower
4 scallions
2 tablespoons oil or melted lard
1 tablespoon cornstarch
1 tablespoon soy sauce
1 teaspoon brown sugar
1 teaspoon salt

Wash and core the kidneys, slice them thinly and soak in the sherry. Break the cauliflower into very small florets. Cook in salted boiling water for 3 minutes. Drain. Cut the spring onions into 2.5 cm/1 inch lengths.

Heat the oil or lard and fry the kidneys and onions with the cauliflower for 2 minutes. Mix the cornflour to a smooth paste with the soy sauce, 2 × 15 ml spoons/2 tablespoons water, the sugar, the remaining sherry and the salt. Add to the pan and cook gently for 3 minutes, stirring all the time. Serve immediately.

Left: Lamb and vermicelli
Right: Kidney with spring onions (scallions) and cauliflower

Chicken Chop Suey

Metric/Imperial

4 dried mushrooms
150 g/5 oz bamboo shoots
1 onion
1 pepper
0.5 kg/1 lb bean sprouts
350 g/12 oz cooked chicken
2 × 15 ml spoons/2 tablespoons peanut oil
300 ml/½ pint chicken stock
1 × 2.5 ml spoon/½ teaspoon sugar
1 × 5 ml spoon/1 teaspoon soy sauce
salt
pepper
1 × 5 ml spoon/1 teaspoon cornflour
1 × 15 ml spoon/1 tablespoon dry sherry

American

4 dried mushrooms
2 cups bamboo shoots
1 onion
1 pepper
8 cups bean sprouts
3 cups cooked chicken
2 tablespoons peanut oil
1¼ cups chicken stock
½ teaspoon sugar
1 teaspoon soy sauce
salt
pepper
1 teaspoon cornstarch
1 tablespoon dry sherry

Soak the mushrooms in warm water for 20 minutes, rinse, squeeze dry and cut into thin slices, discarding the stalks. Cut the bamboo shoots into thin strips. Cut the onion into eight. Slice the pepper thinly. Drain the bean sprouts, rinse in cold running water and drain again. Cut the chicken into 1 cm/½ inch cubes.

Heat the oil in a saucepan and add the chicken and vegetables. Cook, stirring, for 3 to 4 minutes. Add the stock, sugar, soy sauce and seasonings, bring to the boil, stirring constantly and simmer for 5 minutes. Mix the cornflour with the sherry and add to the saucepan. Bring to the boil, stirring constantly, and cook for a further 3 minutes.

Chicken Livers with Prawns (Shrimp) and Broccoli

Metric/Imperial

225 g/8 oz chicken livers
2 × 15 ml spoons/2 tablespoons cornflour
2 × 15 ml spoons/2 tablespoons oil
75 g/3 oz fresh mushrooms
1 spring onion
pinch of salt
pinch of pepper
350 g/12 oz frozen broccoli
100 g/4 oz peeled prawns
1 × 5 ml spoon/1 teaspoon cornflour
1 × 15 ml spoon/1 tablespoon soy sauce

American

½ lb chicken livers
2 tablespoons cornstarch
2 tablespoons oil
1 cup fresh mushrooms
1 scallion
pinch of salt
pinch of pepper
¾ lb frozen broccoli
¼ lb peeled shrimps
1 teaspoon cornstarch
1 tablespoon soy sauce

Wash and dry the chicken livers, slice thinly and toss in 2 tablespoons cornflour. Heat oil and fry livers for 1 minute. Wash and dry the mushrooms, slice thinly, add to the pan and cook for 1 minute. Chop the onion finely and add to the pan with the salt and pepper. Mix well. Cook the broccoli in salted boiling water for 5 minutes. Drain and add to the pan with the prawns.

Mix the remaining cornflour to a smooth paste with the soy sauce and 5 × 15 ml spoons/5 tablespoons water. Add to the pan. Bring to the boil, stirring until slightly thickened. Cook for 3 minutes. Serve immediately.

Right: Chicken livers with prawns (shrimp) and broccoli

Pork and Mushrooms

Metric/Imperial

0.5 kg/1 lb lean pork
1 × 15 ml spoon/1 tablespoon soy sauce
1 × 15 ml spoon/1 tablespoon sherry
2 × 15 ml spoons/2 tablespoons oil
100 g/4 oz fresh mushrooms
1 × 5 ml spoon/1 teaspoon cornflour
3 × 15 ml spoons/3 tablespoons stock or water

American

1 lb lean pork
1 tablespoon soy sauce
1 tablespoon sherry
2 tablespoons oil
1 cup fresh mushrooms
1 teaspoon cornstarch
3 tablespoons stock or water

Cut the pork into thin slices, add the soy sauce and sherry. Toss well. Heat the oil and fry the meat over a fierce heat, stirring all the time, for 2 minutes. Remove from the pan and keep hot. Wash and dry the mushrooms. Slice them thinly and fry quickly in the remaining oil. Add the meat again and mix well.

Mix the cornflour to a smooth paste with the stock or water, add to the pan and heat gently, stirring all the time until slightly thickened.

Ham and Sweet Peppers

Metric/Imperial

3 sweet peppers
350 g/12 oz ham
1 × 15 ml spoon/1 tablespoon cornflour
2 × 15 ml spoons/2 tablespoons soy sauce
1 × 15 ml spoon/1 tablespoon sherry
1 × 5 ml spoon/1 teaspoon sugar
2 × 15 ml spoons/2 tablespoons stock or water
2 × 15 ml spoons/2 tablespoons oil

Wash the peppers, deseed and cut into 2.5 cm/1 inch pieces. Cover with boiling water for 1 minute; drain. Slice the ham and cut into 2.5 cm/1 inch squares. Mix the cornflour, soy sauce, sherry, sugar and stock or water together, add to the ham and mix well so that the meat is completely coated.

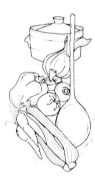

American

3 sweet peppers
¾ lb ham
1 tablespoon cornstarch
2 tablespoons soy sauce
1 tablespoon sherry
1 teaspoon sugar
2 tablespoons stock or water
2 tablespoons oil

Heat the oil and fry the pepper pieces for 2 minutes over a fierce heat, stirring all the time. Remove from the pan. Add the ham to the pan with the liquid, cook for 1 minute, stirring all the time over a medium heat. Add the peppers, cook for a further 1 minute and serve immediately.

Above left: Ham and sweet peppers
Right: Pork and mushrooms

Beef with Broccoli

Metric/Imperial

MARINADE:

2 × 5 ml/2 teaspoons soy sauce
1 × 15 ml spoon/1 tablespoon sherry
1 × 15 ml spoon/1 tablespoon cornflour
1 × 15 ml spoon/1 tablespoon oil

0.5 kg/1 lb beef (sirloin or rib, boned)
0.5 kg/1 lb broccoli
1 × 5 ml spoon/1 teaspoon salt
3 × 15 ml spoons/3 tablespoons oil
2 cloves garlic, crushed
3–4 slices fresh ginger
2 × 5 ml spoons/2 teaspoons sugar
2 × 15 ml spoons/2 tablespoons soy sauce or oyster
  sauce

American

MARINADE:

2 teaspoons soy sauce
1 tablespoon sherry
1 tablespoon cornstarch
1 tablespoon oil

1 lb beef (tenderloin or flank
  steak)
1 lb broccoli
1 teaspoon salt
3 tablespoons oil
2 cloves garlic, crushed
3–4 slices fresh ginger
2 teaspoons sugar
2 tablespoons soy sauce or oyster
  sauce

Mix together the ingredients for the marinade in a large bowl. Slice the beef thinly across the grain into bite sized pieces. Add the beef to the marinade and mix well.

Separate the broccoli florets and slice the stems diagonally. Put the broccoli in a pan of boiling salted water and cook for 1 minute. Remove from the pan and rinse with cold water.

Heat the oil, add the garlic and sliced ginger and stir three or four times. Add the beef and stir fry until the colour changes. Add the broccoli, sugar and soy or oyster sauce. Stir fry for 1 minute and serve immediately.

Beef with Celery and Cabbage

Metric/Imperial

0.5 kg/1 lb rump steak
1 × 5 ml spoon/1 teaspoon cornflour
2 × 15 ml spoons/2 tablespoons oil or melted
  dripping
2 sticks celery
4 spring onions
100 g/4 oz white cabbage
1 × 15 ml spoon/1 tablespoon soy sauce
pinch of salt
pinch of black pepper

American

1 lb rump steak
1 teaspoon cornstarch
2 tablespoons oil or melted
  dripping
2 stalks celery
4 scallions
¼ lb white cabbage
1 tablespoon soy sauce
pinch of salt
pinch of black pepper

Wipe the meat and cut into paper thin slices. Mix the cornflour to a smooth paste with about 2 × 15 ml spoons/2 tablespoons water, add to the beef and mix well until the meat is completely coated. Heat the oil or dripping and fry the meat over a fierce heat, stirring all the time, for 3 minutes. Remove from the pan.

Wash and slice the celery; wash and finely chop the spring onions; wash and shred the cabbage. Add the vegetables to the remaining oil or fat in pan, fry gently for 5 minutes, stirring occasionally. Add the meat, soy sauce, salt and pepper, mix well and cook for 2 to 3 minutes. Serve immediately.

Right: Beef with celery and cabbage

50

Prawn Chop Suey

Metric/Imperial
225 g/8 oz peeled prawns
4 dried mushrooms
0.5 kg/1 lb bean sprouts
100 g/4 oz bamboo shoots
8 water chestnuts
0.5 × 15 ml spoon/½ tablespoon cornflour
pinch of salt
1 × 15 ml spoon/1 tablespoon soy sauce
1 clove garlic, crushed
1 × 5 ml spoon/1 teaspoon sugar
1 × 15 ml spoon/1 tablespoon dry sherry
50 g/2 oz blanched, toasted almonds

American
½ lb peeled shrimps
4 dried mushrooms
8 cups bean sprouts
2 cups bamboo shoots
8 water chestnuts
½ tablespoon cornstarch
pinch of salt
1 tablespoon soy sauce
1 clove garlic, crushed
1 teaspoon sugar
1 tablespoon dry sherry
½ cup blanched, toasted almonds

Cut the prawns in half if large. Soak the mushrooms in warm water for 20 minutes, rinse, squeeze dry and slice, discarding the stalks. Rinse the bean sprouts under running cold water and drain. Cut the bamboo shoots and water chestnuts into matchstick strips.

Mix the cornflour, salt, soy sauce, garlic, sugar, sherry, vegetables and 4 × 15 ml spoons/4 tablespoons/⅓ cup water in a small saucepan. Bring to the boil and simmer slowly, stirring for 2 to 3 minutes. Stir in the prawns, cover the pan and cook gently until the prawns are hot through. Serve on a heated dish, topped with the almonds.

Onion and Ginger Crab with Egg Sauce

Metric/Imperial
2–3 medium crabs
2 × 5 ml spoons/2 teaspoons salt
4–5 slices fresh ginger, shredded
2 × 15 ml spoons/2 tablespoons soy sauce
1 × 15 ml spoon/1 tablespoon chilli sauce
2 × 15 ml spoons/2 tablespoons dry sherry
150 ml/¼ pint clear broth (page 00)
3–4 spring onions
5 × 15 ml spoons/5 tablespoons vegetable oil
2 onions, sliced thinly
4 cloves garlic, crushed
1 egg, beaten

American
2–3 medium crabs
2 teaspoons salt
4–5 slices fresh ginger, shredded
2 tablespoons soy sauce
1 tablespoon chili sauce
2 tablespoons dry sherry
⅔ cup clear broth (page 82)
3–4 scallions
⅓ cup vegetable oil
2 onions, sliced thinly
4 cloves garlic, crushed
1 egg, beaten

Separate the large main shell from the body of each crab by inserting a knife under the shell as a lever. Crack the claws and shells. Chop each body into quarters (leaving a leg or two attached to use as a 'handle' when eating). Remove and discard all the spongy parts. Rub all over the crab bodies with the salt and ginger.

Mix the soy sauce, chilli sauce, sherry and broth until they are well blended. Trim the spring onions and cut into 2.5 cm/1 inch lengths.

Heat the oil in a large frying pan over high heat. When it is hot add the onions and garlic. Stir fry for 30 seconds. Add all the crab pieces and stir fry for 3 to 4 minutes until well cooked through. Add the spring onions then pour the broth sauce over the crab pieces. As the sauce boils and froths up, pour the egg in a thin stream over the crab pieces and stir fry for a further 1½ minutes.

Turn the mixture on to a warmed dish. Eat by scraping the crab meat out of the main shells or holding on to one of the legs and chewing and sucking the meat out of the body.

Above: Fried lobster with bean sprouts

Fried Lobster with Bean Sprouts

Metric/Imperial
225 g/8 oz lobster meat
pinch of salt
pinch of black pepper
1 × 15 ml spoon/1 tablespoon oil or melted lard
0.5 kg/1 lb bean sprouts
1 × 5 ml spoon/1 teaspoon cornflour
1 × 5 ml spoon/1 teaspoon brown sugar
3 × 15 ml spoons/3 tablespoons water
1 × 15 ml spoon/1 tablespoon soy sauce
1 spring onion

Cut the lobster into neat slices and season with salt and pepper. Heat the oil or lard and fry the lobster for 1 minute. Wash and drain the bean sprouts, then add to the pan, stirring for 1 minute over a fierce heat.

American
½ lb lobster meat
pinch of salt
pinch of black pepper
1 tablespoon oil or melted lard
8 cups bean sprouts
1 teaspoon cornstarch
1 teaspoon brown sugar
3 tablespoons water
1 tablespoon soy sauce
1 scallion

Mix the cornflour and sugar together to a smooth paste with the water and soy sauce. Add to the pan and heat gently, stirring until slightly thickened. Chop the spring onion (scallion) finely, add to the pan and mix well. Serve immediately.

Woolly Lamb

Metric/Imperial

0.5 kg/1 lb leg or shoulder of lamb
150 g/5 oz bamboo shoots
1 onion
1 carrot
2 dried mushrooms
2 × 15 ml spoons/2 tablespoons peanut oil
1 × 2.5 ml spoon/½ teaspoon salt
300 ml/½ pint chicken stock
1 × 15 ml spoon/1 tablespoon soy sauce
1 × 2.5 ml spoon/½ teaspoon sugar
2 × 15 ml spoons/2 tablespoons cornflour
50 g/2 oz transparent noodles
oil for deep frying

American

1 lb leg or shoulder of lamb
5 oz bamboo shoots
1 onion
1 carrot
2 dried mushrooms
2 tablespoons peanut oil
½ teaspoon salt
1¼ cups chicken stock
1 tablespoon soy sauce
½ teaspoon sugar
2 tablespoons cornstarch
1 cup transparent noodles
oil for deep frying

Cut the lamb into thin slices and the bamboo shoots into thin strips. Cut the onion into eight and the carrot into wedges. Soak the mushrooms in warm water for 20 minutes, rinse, squeeze dry and slice, discarding the stalks.

Heat the oil in a saucepan and fry the meat until it changes colour. Pour off the excess oil and add the prepared vegetables, salt, stock, soy sauce, sugar and cornflour. Bring to the boil and simmer, stirring constantly, for 5 minutes. Loosen the transparent noodles and deep fry in hot oil until they puff up, about 15 seconds. Drain well on absorbent kitchen paper.

Serve the lamb mixture on a heated serving plate, topped with the noodles.

Note: This dish owes its name and spectacular appearance to the transparent noodles but 100 g/4 oz ordinary dried egg noodles could be substituted if transparent noodles are not available. These should be boiled in water for 5 minutes, then drained and deep fried.

Duck with Almonds

Metric/Imperial

0.5 kg/1 lb duck meat
2 × 15 ml spoons/2 tablespoons oil
1 × 5 ml spoon/1 teaspoon salt
2 × 15 ml spoons/2 tablespoons soy sauce
2 sticks celery
50 g/2 oz fresh mushrooms
100 g/4 oz shelled peas
300 ml/½ pint stock
2 × 5 ml spoons/2 teaspoons cornflour
75 g/3 oz split, roasted almonds

American

1 lb duck meat
2 tablespoons oil
1 teaspoon salt
2 tablespoons soy sauce
2 stalks celery
½ cup fresh mushrooms
¾ cup shelled peas
1¼ cups stock
2 teaspoons cornstarch
¾ cup split, roasted almonds

Cut the duck meat into paper thin slices. Heat the oil, add the salt and duck and fry for about 5 minutes or until the meat is tender. Add the soy sauce and mix well.

Wash and chop the celery. Wash and thinly slice the mushrooms. Add both to the pan with the peas, mix well and cook for 1 minute. Add the stock, bring to the boil and simmer for 5 minutes. Mix the cornflour to a smooth paste with a little cold water, stir into the pan; bring to the boil, stirring all the time, and cook until slightly thickened. Add the almonds and serve immediately.

Right: Duck with almonds

Prawns (Shrimp) with Vegetables

Metric/Imperial

0.5 kg/1 lb prawns
1 red pepper
2 sticks celery
2 dried mushrooms
2 spring onions
6 water chestnuts
1 × 15 ml spoon/1 tablespoon cornflour
1 × 15 ml spoon/1 tablespoon soy sauce
pinch of sugar
1 × 15 ml spoon/1 tablespoon peanut oil
1 × 2.5 ml spoon/½ teaspoon very finely chopped
  fresh ginger
1 clove garlic, crushed
1 × 2.5 ml spoon/½ teaspoon salt
2 pineapple rings, chopped (optional)
300 ml/½ pint chicken stock
25 g/1 oz flaked, toasted almonds

American

1 lb shrimp
1 red pepper
2 stalks celery
2 dried mushrooms
2 scallions
6 water chestnuts
1 tablespoon cornstarch
1 tablespoon soy sauce
pinch of sugar
1 tablespoon peanut oil
½ teaspoon very finely chopped
  fresh ginger
1 clove garlic, crushed
½ teaspoon salt
2 pineapple rings, chopped
  (optional)
1¼ cups chicken stock
¼ cup flaked, toasted almonds

Peel the prawns. If using large ones, devein and cut them in half. Cut the pepper into matchstick strips and slice the celery diagonally. Soak the mushrooms in warm water for 20 minutes, rinse, squeeze dry and slice, discarding the stalks. Cut the spring onions into 1 cm/½ inch lengths and slice the water chestnuts. Mix the cornflour to a smooth paste with the soy sauce, sugar and 2 × 15 ml spoons/2 tablespoons water.

Heat the oil and add the ginger, garlic and salt. Add the prepared vegetables, pineapple and stock. Bring to the boil and simmer, stirring, for 5 minutes. Add the cornflour mixture and cook, stirring, for 2 to 3 minutes. Add the prawns and allow to heat through. Serve in a hot serving dish, scattered with flaked, toasted almonds.

Sweet and Sour Prawns (Shrimp)

Metric/Imperial

225 g/8 oz peeled prawns
1 × 15 ml spoon/1 tablespoon sherry
salt
pepper
1 onion
1 green pepper
1 × 15 ml spoon/1 tablespoon peanut oil
0.5 × 425 g/½ × 15 oz can pineapple chunks
1 × 15 ml spoon/1 tablespoon cornflour
1 × 15 ml spoon/1 tablespoon soy sauce
150 ml/¼ pint vinegar
4 × 15 ml spoons/4 tablespoons brown sugar

American

½ lb peeled shrimps
1 tablespoon sherry
salt
pepper
1 onion
1 green pepper
1 tablespoon peanut oil
½ × 15 oz can pineapple chunks
1 tablespoon cornstarch
1 tablespoon soy sauce
⅔ cup vinegar
¼ cup brown sugar

Put the prawns in a bowl with the sherry, salt and pepper and marinate for 1 hour. Slice the onion and cut the pepper into wedges. Heat the oil in a small saucepan, add the vegetables and fry gently until softened. Add the pineapple.

Mix together the cornflour, soy sauce, vinegar and sugar and add to the saucepan. Bring to the boil, stirring constantly, and simmer for 2 to 3 minutes. Add the prawns and sherry and cook until the prawns are hot through. Serve in a heated dish.

Right: Prawns (shrimp) with vegetables

Shallow and deep frying

The Chinese also fry without stirring, much as we do in the West. For this type of dish the food will more often than not be coated with a batter or some other mixture that will give a crisp outer 'skin' to the food.

Crisp Skin Fish

Metric/Imperial

4 whiting
100 g/4 oz peeled prawns
1 spring onion
4 dried mushrooms
*1 × 5 ml spoon/1 teaspoon very finely chopped
   fresh ginger*
salt
1 egg yolk
cornflour
oil for frying
SAUCE:
1 × 15 ml spoon/1 tablespoon vinegar
1 × 15 ml spoon/1 tablespoon sugar
2 × 15 ml spoons/2 tablespoons salted black beans
1 × 15 ml spoon/1 tablespoon cornflour
150ml/¼ pint fish stock or water
1 × 15 ml spoon/1 tablespoon soy sauce
salt

American

4 whiting
¼ lb peeled shrimps
1 scallion
4 dried mushrooms
*1 teaspoon very finely chopped
   fresh ginger*
salt
1 egg yolk
cornstarch
oil for frying
SAUCE:
1 tablespoon vinegar
1 tablespoon sugar
2 tablespoons salted black beans
1 tablespoon cornstarch
⅔ cup fish stock or water
1 tablespoon soy sauce
salt

Clean the fish, leaving on the heads and tails. Chop the prawns and spring onions. Soak the mushrooms for 20 minutes in warm water, rinse, squeeze dry and chop, discarding the stalks. Mix the prawns, mushrooms, spring onions and ginger and stuff the fish with this mixture. Sew up the openings. Cut gashes on both sides of each fish, in the thickest part, and rub salt into the flesh.

Beat the egg yolk with 1 × 5 ml spoon/1 teaspoon water and brush it over the fish. Leave to dry then rub over the cornflour. Heat about 5 cm/2 inches oil in a pan and fry the fish, turning once. When cooked, drain on absorbent kitchen paper. Keep hot.

Put all the remaining ingredients in a small saucepan. Bring to the boil, stirring constantly, and simmer for 2 to 3 minutes. Put the fish on a hot serving dish, and pour the sauce over.

Sesame Fish

Metric/Imperial

0.5 kg/1 lb fish fillets
1 onion, chopped finely
*1 × 5 ml spoon/1 teaspoon very finely chopped
   fresh ginger*
2 × 15 ml spoons/2 tablespoons dry sherry
1 × 2.5 ml spoon/½ teaspoon salt
pinch of pepper
1 × 5 ml spoon/1 teaspoon sugar
25 g/1 oz cornflour
25 g/1 oz plain flour
1 egg
sesame seeds
oil for deep frying

American

1 lb fish fillets
1 onion, chopped finely
*1 teaspoon very finely chopped
   fresh ginger*
2 tablespoons dry sherry
½ teaspoon salt
pinch of pepper
1 teaspoon sugar
¼ cup cornstarch
¼ cup all-purpose flour
1 egg
sesame seeds
oil for deep frying

Skin the fish and cut it into bite-sized pieces. Mix the onion with the ginger, sherry, salt, pepper and sugar. Add the fish pieces and marinate for 10 minutes, stirring occasionally. Drain.

Sift the cornflour and flour into a bowl. Add the egg and 3 × 15 ml spoons/3 tablespoons water and mix well. Dip the fish in this batter, then in sesame seeds. Deep fry in hot oil until crisp and golden. Serve hot.

Right: Crisp skin fish

Prawn Balls

Metric/Imperial
100 g/4 oz self-raising flour
pinch of salt
1 egg
150 ml/¼ pint water
0.5 kg/1 lb peeled prawns
2 × 15 ml spoons/2 tablespoons cornflour
1 × 2.5 ml spoon/½ teaspoon salt
1 × 2.5 ml spoon/½ teaspoon white pepper
pinch of monosodium glutamate
oil for deep frying

American
1 cup self-rising flour
pinch of salt
1 egg
⅔ cup water
1 lb peeled shrimps
2 tablespoons cornstarch
½ teaspoon salt
½ teaspoon white pepper
pinch of monosodium glutamate
oil for deep frying

Sift the flour and salt into a bowl. Make a well in the centre and add the egg. Using a wooden spoon, mix the flour into the egg, add half the water and continue mixing, drawing in the flour from round the sides of the bowl. Beat thoroughly and stir in the remaining water.

Cut the prawns into chunks about 2.5 cm/1 inch across. Mix the cornflour with the remaining salt, pepper and monosodium glutamate. Coat the prawn pieces in the seasoned cornflour, dip them in batter and fry in deep, hot oil until crisp and golden. Drain well on absorbent kitchen paper. Serve plain or with a sweet and sour sauce.

Prawn Cutlets

Metric/Imperial
8 Mediterranean (very large) prawns
1 × 15 ml spoon/1 tablespoon sherry
1 egg
2 × 15 ml spoons/2 tablespoons cornflour
oil for deep frying

American
4 Pacific shrimps
1 tablespoon sherry
1 egg
2 tablespoons cornstarch
oil for deep frying

Hold the prawns firmly by the tail and remove the rest of the shell, leaving the tail piece intact. Split the prawns in half lengthways almost to the tail and remove the intestinal cord. Flatten the prawns to look like cutlets. Sprinkle with sherry.

Beat the egg and dip the cutlets in it, then coat them in cornflour. Do this twice to give a good thick coating. Fry the cutlets in deep oil for 2 to 3 minutes and drain on absorbent kitchen paper. Serve plain or with sweet and sour sauce.

Below: Prawn (shrimp) balls
Right: Prawn (shrimp) cutlets

Pineapple Fish

Metric/Imperial

0.5 kg/1 lb fish fillet (eg. haddock), or
   2 × 200 g/7 oz cans tuna
100 g/4 oz self-raising flour
salt
1 egg
300 ml/½ pint water
pinch of monosodium glutamate
4 pineapple rings
2 × 15 ml spoons/2 tablespoons soft brown sugar
1 × 15 ml spoon/1 tablespoon cornflour
2 × 15 ml spoons/2 tablespoons vinegar
1 × 15 ml spoon/1 tablespoon soy sauce
1 × 5 ml spoon/1 teaspoon very finely chopped
   fresh ginger
150 ml/¼ pint syrup from canned pineapple
oil for deep frying
toasted flaked almonds to garnish

American

1 lb fish fillet (eg. snapper), or
   2 × 7 oz cans tuna
1 cup self-rising flour
salt
1 egg
1¼ cups water
pinch of monosodium glutamate
4 pineapple rings
2 tablespoons soft brown sugar
1 tablespoon cornstarch
2 tablespoons vinegar
1 tablespoon soy sauce
1 teaspoon very finely chopped
   fresh ginger
⅔ cup syrup from canned
   pineapple
oil for deep frying
toasted flaked almonds to garnish

Skin the fish and cut it into bite-sized pieces or drain the tuna and break into bite-sized pieces. Sift the flour and a pinch of salt together into a bowl. Make a well in the centre, add the egg and mix with a little flour, using a wooden spoon. Gradually add half the water, then the rest of the flour and beat until the batter is smooth. Beat in the monosodium glutamate.

Chop the pineapple roughly. Mix together the brown sugar, cornflour, vinegar, soy sauce, ginger, pineapple syrup, a little salt and the remaining water. Bring to the boil, stirring, and boil for 2 to 3 minutes.

Dip the fish pieces in batter and fry in deep hot oil until crisp and golden. Drain on absorbent kitchen paper. Add the pineapple pieces to the sauce and reheat. Sprinkle the fish with the toasted flaked almonds and serve in a hot serving bowl with the sauce poured over.

Below: Sweet and sour pork with lychees (page 64)
Right: Pineapple fish

Sweet and Sour Pork with Lychees

Metric/Imperial

0.5 kg/1 lb shoulder of pork
4 × 15 ml spoons/4 tablespoons soy sauce
1 × 15 ml spoon/1 tablespoon dry sherry
1 × 5 ml spoon/1 teaspoon very finely chopped
   fresh ginger
pinch of monosodium glutamate
25 g/1 oz plain flour
4 × 15 ml spoons/4 tablespoons cornflour
salt
2 eggs, beaten
oil for deep frying
½ red pepper
½ green pepper
2 apples
1 × 15 ml spoon/1 tablespoon brown sugar
150 ml/¼ pint syrup from canned lychees
2 × 15 ml spoons/2 tablespoons vinegar
4 spring onions, finely chopped
1 × 300/11 oz can lychees, drained

American

1 lb shoulder of pork
⅓ cup soy sauce
1 tablespoon dry sherry
1 teaspoon very finely chopped
   fresh ginger
pinch of monosodium glutamate
¼ cup all-purpose flour
¼ cup cornstarch
salt
2 eggs, beaten
oil for deep frying
½ red pepper
½ green pepper
2 apples
1 tablespoon brown sugar
⅔ cup syrup from canned lychees
2 tablespoons vinegar
4 scallions, finely chopped
1 × 11 oz can lychees, drained

Cut the pork into 2.5 cm/1 inch cubes. Mix together in a bowl 3 × 15 ml spoons/3 tablespoons soy sauce, the sherry, ginger and monosodium glutamate. Add the pork, stir until the meat is coated. Leave to marinate for 1 to 2 hours.

Sift the flour, 3 × 15 ml spoons/3 tablespoons cornflour and a pinch of salt into a bowl. Add the eggs gradually, beating well, to make a smooth batter. Coat the pork cubes in batter and deep fry in hot oil until golden. Drain on absorbent kitchen paper and keep hot.

Cut the peppers into wedges. Peel, core and quarter the apples. Mix with all the remaining ingredients in a small saucepan; add salt to taste. Bring to the boil, stirring constantly, and simmer for 2 to 3 minutes.

Serve the pork on a heated dish and pour the sauce over.

Fish Rolls with Walnuts

Metric/Imperial

2 large fish fillets (eg. John Dory, plaice or sole)
2 spring onions
1 × 2.5 ml spoon/½ teaspoon salt
1 × 2.5 spoon/½ teaspoon sugar
1 × 2.5 ml spoon/½ teaspoon cornflour
1 × 5 ml spoon/1 teaspoon soy sauce
1 × 5 ml spoon/1 teaspoon dry sherry
1 egg
50 g/2 oz finely chopped walnuts
2 × 25 g/1 oz slices cooked ham
oil for deep frying

American

2 large fish fillets (eg. flounder,
   sole)
2 scallions
½ teaspoon salt
½ teaspoon sugar
½ teaspoon cornstarch
1 teaspoon soy sauce
1 teaspoon dry sherry
1 egg
½ cup finely chopped or ground
   walnuts
2 × 1 oz slices cooked ham
oil for deep frying

Cut the fillets into quarters, making 8 even-sized pieces. Chop the spring onions finely, mix with the salt, sugar, cornflour, soy sauce, sherry and egg and beat together well.

Dip the fish pieces in the egg mixture and then in the walnuts. Cut each slice of ham in quarters and lay a quarter on each piece of fish. Roll up and secure with wooden cocktail sticks. Deep fry in hot oil until golden. Drain well on absorbent kitchen paper and serve very hot.

Right: Fish rolls with walnuts

Sweet and Sour Chicken Drumsticks

Metric/Imperial

6 chicken drumsticks
1 egg
5 × 15 ml spoons/5 tablespoons cornflour
salt
pepper
1 onion
1 small pepper
1 carrot
450 ml/¾ pint chicken stock
4 × 15 ml spoons/4 tablespoons vinegar
4 × 15 ml spoons/4 tablespoons soft brown sugar
1 × 15 ml spoon/1 tablespoon soy sauce
1 × 15 ml spoon/1 tablespoon sherry (optional)
oil for deep frying

American

6 chicken drumsticks
1 egg
⅓ cup cornstarch
salt
pepper
1 onion
1 small pepper
1 carrot
2 cups chicken stock
⅓ cup vinegar
¼ cup soft brown sugar
1 tablespoon soy sauce
1 tablespoon sherry (optional)
oil for deep frying

Trim the drumsticks if necessary. Beat the egg with 1 × 15 ml spoon/1 tablespoon water. Mix 4 × 15 ml spoons/4 tablespoons/¼ cup cornflour with a little salt and pepper. Dip the drumsticks in the egg, then in the seasoned cornflour and put to one side.

Cut the onion into eight and the pepper and carrot into wedges. Drop these into a small saucepan of boiling water and cook for 5 minutes. Drain well. Mix together in a small saucepan the remaining cornflour and the stock, vinegar, sugar, soy sauce and sherry. Bring to the boil, stirring constantly, and simmer for 2 to 3 minutes.

Heat the oil and deep fry the chicken drumsticks until golden and tender. Drain on absorbent kitchen paper. Add the vegetables to the sauce, then add the chicken and reheat. Serve very hot.

Uncooked dishes

Some foods can be made tender and tasty with no cooking at all. This is generally done by marinating, as in this dish of raw fish.

Raw Fish Strips

Metric/Imperial

0.5 kg/1 lb plaice fillets
1 spring onion
1 × 15 ml spoon/1 tablespoon sesame oil
2 × 15 ml spoons/2 tablespoons sherry
2 × 15 ml spoons/2 tablespoons soy sauce
pinch of salt
pinch of black pepper
1 slice pineapple

American

1 lb flounder fillets
1 scallion
1 tablespoon sesame oil
2 tablespoons sherry
2 tablespoons soy sauce
pinch of salt
pinch of black pepper
1 slice pineapple

Skin the fish and cut it into narrow strips about 5 cm/2 inches long. Chop the spring onion very finely and put it in a shallow dish with all the other ingredients, except the pineapple. Add the fish and toss well in the mixture. Leave for 10 minutes.

Lift the fish out of the marinade. Shred the pineapple finely and mix it with the fish. Serve piled on a large plate.

Right: Sweet and sour chicken drumsticks

Quick roasting

Traditional Chinese quick roasting (cha shao) is preceded by seasoning and marinating the raw meat or fish. Roasting at a very high temperature for 10 to 15 minutes produces a rich, highly seasoned crust round the meat; cooking can then continue at a slightly lower temperature until the food is cooked through. This is an ideal method of cooking a tender joint or whole fish or poultry.

Red Roast Pork

Metric/Imperial

0.5 kg/1 lb pork fillet
1 × 15 ml spoon/1 tablespoon hoisin sauce
1 × 5 ml spoon/1 teaspoon five-spice powder
1 × 15 ml spoon/1 tablespoon soy sauce
0.5 × 15 ml spoon/½ tablespoon soft brown sugar
1 clove garlic, crushed
1 × 5 ml spoon/1 teaspoon very finely chopped
   fresh ginger
peanut oil

American

1 lb pork tenderloin
1 tablespoon hoisin sauce
1 teaspoon five-spice powder
1 tablespoon soy sauce
½ tablespoon soft brown sugar
1 clove garlic, crushed
1 teaspoon very finely chopped
   fresh ginger
peanut oil

Trim the pork but leave it in one piece. Mix together all the remaining ingredients except the oil and combine them thoroughly. Place the meat in a dish, brush it with oil and then coat it in the sauce. Leave to marinade for 1 to 2 hours.

Spoon more oil over the pork, place it on a rack in the roasting tin and roast in a preheated, hot oven (220°C/425°F/Gas Mark 7) for 10 minutes. Reduce the oven temperature to moderate (180°C/350°F/Gas Mark 4) and cook for a further 30 to 35 minutes. Cut the pork in slices diagonally and serve on a hot plate.

Cha Shao Quick-roast Pork with Cabbage

Metric/Imperial

0.75 kg/1½ lb pork fillet
1 small cabbage
1 × 15 ml spoon/1 tablespoon butter
½ chicken stock cube
1 × 15 ml spoon/1 tablespoon soy sauce
salt, pepper
5–6 × 15 ml spoons/5–6 tablespoons water
MARINADE:
1.5 × 15 ml spoons/1½ tablespoons soy sauce
1 × 15 ml spoon/1 tablespoon hoisin sauce or soy
   paste
1.5 × 5 ml spoons/1½ teaspoons soy jam
1 × 2.5 spoon/½ teaspoon salt
1.5 × 15 ml spoons/1½ tablespoons vegetable oil
1.5 × 5 ml spoons/1½ teaspoons sugar

American

1½ lb pork tenderloin
1 small cabbage
1 tablespoon butter
½ chicken bouillon cube
1 tablespoon soy sauce
salt, pepper
5–6 tablespoons water
MARINADE:
1½ tablespoons soy sauce
1 tablespoon hoisin sauce or soy
   paste
1½ teaspoons soy jam
½ teaspoon salt
1½ tablespoons vegetable oil
1½ teaspoons sugar

Mix all the marinade ingredients until they are well blended. Add the pork and baste well. Leave for 2 to 2½ hours, turning the pork every 30 minutes. Shred the cabbage.

Arrange the pork a rack in a roasting pan and put into the oven, preheated to 230–240°C/ 450–475°F/Gas Mark 8–9. Roast for 12 to 14 minutes, turning once. Remove the pork from the oven and keep it hot.

Put the roasting pan (with the drippings) over moderate heat and add the butter. When the fat is melted add the cabbage. Stir and turn to coat well. Sprinkle the cabbage with the crumbled stock cube, soy sauce, salt, pepper and water. Increase the heat to fairly high, cover and cook for 2 to 3 minutes, adding more water if necessary.

To serve, cut the pork across the grain into thin slices. Arrange it on a bed of hot cooked rice and top with the cabbage and sauce.

Right: Red roast pork

Cha Shao Fish with Leeks and Tomatoes

Metric/Imperial	American
MARINADE:	MARINADE:
1.5 × 15 ml spoons/1½ tablespoons soy sauce	1½ tablespoons soy sauce
1 × 15 ml spoon/1 tablespoon hoisin sauce or soy paste	1 tablespoon hoisin sauce or soy paste
1.5 × 5 ml spoon/1½ teaspoons soy jam (optional)	1½ teaspoons soy jam (optional)
1 × 2.5 ml spoon/½ teaspoon salt	½ teaspoon salt
1.5 × 15 ml spoons/1½ tablespoons vegetable oil	1½ tablespoons vegetable oil
1.5 × 5 ml spoons/1½ teaspoons sugar	1½ teaspoons sugar

Metric/Imperial	American
1 kg/2 lb chunky fish, such as cod, haddock, carp, bream	2 lb chunky fish, such as cod, haddock, carp bream
2 slices fresh ginger, chopped	2 slices fresh ginger, chopped
3 leeks	3 leeks
3 tomatoes	3 tomatoes
1.5 × 15 ml spoons/1½ tablespoons butter	1½ tablespoons butter
½ chicken stock cube	½ chicken bouillon cube
1 × 5 ml spoon/1 teaspoon sugar	1 teaspoon sugar
1 × 15 ml spoon/1 tablespoon soy sauce	1 tablespoon soy sauce
2 × 15 ml spoons/2 tablespoons dry sherry	2 tablespoons dry sherry

Mix together all the ingredients for the marinade until they are well blended. Cut the fish into four to six pieces. Sprinkle with the chopped ginger, add to the marinade and baste well. Leave for 1 hour, basting occasionally.

Clean the leeks thoroughly and cut into 1 cm/½ inch lengths. Cut the tomatoes into quarters.

Arrange the fish pieces on a rack in the roasting tin and roast in a preheated oven (230–240°C/450–475°F/Gas Mark 8–9) for 10 to 12 minutes, turning once. Remove the fish from the oven and keep it hot. Melt the butter in the roasting tin over moderate heat. Add the leeks and tomatoes, stir and turn to coat well. Sprinkle with the crumbled stock cube, sugar, 5–6 × 15 ml spoons/5–6 tablespoons water, the soy sauce and sherry. Increase the heat to fairly high, cover and cook for 2 minutes, adding more water if necessary.

Serve the fish and vegetables spooned over a dish of hot boiled rice.

Below: Cha shao fish with leeks and tomatoes

Above: Cha shao beef with leeks

Cha Shao Beef with Leeks

Metric/Imperial
marinade (as above)
0.75 kg/1½ lb fillet of beef
2 slices fresh ginger
3 leeks
1.5 × 15 ml spoons/1½ tablespoons butter
½ chicken stock cube
1 × 15 ml spoon/1 tablespoon soy sauce
1 × 5 ml spoon/1 teaspoon sugar

Prepare the marinade first. Cut the beef lengthways into two pieces. Peel and grate the ginger, sprinkle it over the beef then add to the marinade and baste well. Leave for 1 hour. Clean the leeks and cut into 1 cm/½ inch lengths.

Arrange the beef pieces on a rack in a roasting tin. Roast in a preheated very hot oven (230–240°C/450–475°F/Gas Mark 8–9) for 10 to 11 minutes, turning once. Remove the beef from the oven and keep hot.

American
marinade (as above)
1½ lb fillet of beef
2 slices fresh ginger
3 leeks
1¼ tablespoons butter
½ chicken bouillon cube
1 tablespoon soy sauce
1 teaspoon sugar

Put the roasting tin over moderate heat and add the butter. When the butter has melted add the leeks. Stir and turn to coat well. Sprinkle with the crumbled stock cube, soy sauce, 5–6 × 15 ml spoons/5–6 tablespoons water and the sugar. Increase the heat to fairly high, cover and cook for 2 minutes, adding more water if necessary.

Cut each piece of beef across the grain into 1 cm/½ inch thick slices. Serve on a bed of hot boiled rice, with the leeks and sauce spooned over.

Quick steaming

Fish, shellfish and eggs are often cooked by quick steaming. All the ingredients are put in the steamer together and the food is served in the cooking dish.

Since there is no added liquid or fat to dilute or alter the flavour of the food, the basic ingredients must be absolutely fresh and of the highest quality.

Steamed Lobster

Metric/Imperial

$1-1\frac{1}{2}$ kg/2–3 lb cooked lobster
2×5 ml spoons/2 teaspoons salt
1×2.5 ml spoon/$\frac{1}{2}$ teaspoon monosodium
   glutamate (optional)
3 cloves garlic, crushed
1×15 ml spoon/1 tablespoon sherry
1×15 ml spoon/1 tablespoon oil
2 onions, sliced thinly
DIP:
4 spring onions
4–5 slices fresh ginger, shredded
1×15 ml spoon/1 tablespoon sugar
4×15 ml spoons/4 tablespoons soy sauce
4×15 ml spoons/4 tablespoons wine vinegar
2×15 ml spoons/2 tablespoons dry sherry

American

2–3 lb cooked lobster
2 teaspoons salt
$\frac{1}{2}$ teaspoon monosodium glutamate
   (optional)
3 cloves garlic, crushed
1 tablespoon dry sherry
1 tablespoon oil
2 onions, sliced thinly
DIP:
4 scallions
4–5 slices fresh ginger, shredded
1 tablespoon sugar
$\frac{1}{3}$ cup soy sauce
$\frac{1}{3}$ cup wine vinegar
2 tablespoons dry sherry

Cut the body of the lobster in half. Remove and discard any black matter and spongy parts. Leave the red coral. Cut each half into three or four sections, depending on size. Rub all over with salt, monosodium glutamate, garlic, sherry and oil. Leave for 30 minutes.

Arrange the sliced onions over the bottom of a large, heatproof dish. Put the lobster pieces on top.

Put the dish in a steamer and steam vigorously for 9 to 10 minutes. Cut the spring onions into 2.5 cm/1 inch lengths and mix all the dip ingredients until well blended. Pour into two small dishes.

Serve the lobster in the cooking dish and put a dish of dip on either side for guests to help themselves.

Steamed Beef with Rice

Metric/Imperial

0.5 kg/1 lb rump steak
8 water chestnuts
100 g/4 oz fresh mushrooms
25 g/1 oz fresh ginger
50 g/2 oz bamboo shoots
1×5 ml spoon/1 teaspoon sherry
1×5 ml spoon/1 teaspoon brown sugar
1×15 ml spoon/1 tablespoon soy sauce
1×5 ml spoon/1 teaspoon salt
1×5 ml spoon/1 teaspoon sesame oil
0.5 kg/1 lb long grain rice
4 eggs

American

1 lb rump steak
8 water chestnuts
$\frac{1}{4}$ lb fresh mushrooms
1 oz fresh ginger
2 oz bamboo shoots
1 teaspoon sherry
1 teaspoon brown sugar
1 tablespoon soy sauce
1 teaspoon salt
1 teaspoon sesame oil
$2\frac{1}{4}$ cups long grain rice
4 eggs

Wipe the meat and mince it finely; chop the chestnuts finely; wash and thinly slice the mushrooms; shred the ginger and bamboo shoots. Mix them all together. Add sherry, sugar, soy sauce, salt and sesame oil and beat well until blended.

Cook the rice in boiling salted water for 10

minutes. Drain well. Spoon it into a greased dish and spread the meat mixture on top. Steam in a steamer or a saucepan half-filled with boiling water for 15 minutes. Break the eggs on top of the beef and steam for a further 10 minutes or until the egg whites are set. Serve from the cooking dish.

Above: Steamed lobster

Steamed Eggs with Salt Eggs, Pickled Eggs and Quail Eggs

Metric/Imperial

2 eggs (chicken)
1 × 5 ml spoon/1 teaspoon salt
300 ml/½ pint clear broth (page 82)
2 salt eggs
2 pickled eggs
4–5 quail eggs (optional)
1.5 × 15 ml spoons/1¼ tablespoons shredded
smoked ham
1.5 × 15 ml spoons/1¼ tablespoons chopped spring
onions

American

2 eggs (chicken)
1 teaspoon salt
1¼ cups clear broth (page 82)
2 salt eggs
2 pickled eggs
4–5 quail eggs (optional)
1¼ tablespoons shredded smoked
ham
1¼ tablespoons chopped scallions

Break the chicken eggs into a bowl and beat until they are well blended. Add the salt and broth and stir until well blended. Remove the shells from the salt and pickled eggs and cut each into 6 to 8 segments. (Quail eggs usually come with the shells already removed.)

Arrange the salt and pickled egg segments alternately round the edge of a deep-sided heatproof dish. Pour the broth mixture into the centre. Stand the quail eggs in the broth mixture, put the dish into a steamer and steam for 10 to 12 minutes. Sprinkle the top of the quail eggs with the ham and the beaten egg mixture with the spring onion. Steam for a further 3 to 4 minutes. Serve from the cooking dish.

Steamed Five Willow Fish

Metric/Imperial

1 kg/2 lb whole fish, such as trout, bream, carp,
 mullet
2 × 5 ml spoons/2 teaspoons salt
1.5 × 15 ml spoons/1½ tablespoons vegetable oil
6 spring onions
6 slices fresh ginger
1 red pepper
2–3 pieces bamboo shoot
2 small chilli peppers
3 × 15 ml spoons/3 tablespoons lard
3 × 15 ml spoons/3 tablespoons soy sauce
3 × 15 ml spoons/3 tablespoons wine vinegar
1 × 15 ml spoon/1 tablespoon cornflour, mixed
 with 5 × 15 ml spoons/5 tablespoons clear broth
 (page 82)

American

2 lb whole fish, such as trout,
 bream, carp, mullet
2 teaspoons salt
1¼ tablespoons vegetable oil
6 scallions
6 slices fresh ginger
1 red pepper
2–3 pieces bamboo shoot
2 small chili peppers
3 tablespoons lard
3 tablespoons soy sauce
3 tablespoons wine vinegar
1 tablespoon cornstarch, mixed
 with ⅓ cup clear broth
 (page 82)

Rub the fish, inside and out, with the salt and oil
and leave for 30 minutes. Cut the spring onions into
5 cm/2 inch lengths and shred the ginger. Discard
the pith and seeds from the pepper and shred the
flesh. Shred the bamboo shoot and the chilli
peppers, discarding the seeds. Arrange the fish in an
oval heatproof serving dish and put the dish in a
steamer. Steam vigorously for 15 minutes. Melt the
lard in a frying pan over moderate heat, add the
chilli peppers and stir and turn in the hot fat a few
times. Add all the vegetables, the soy sauce and
vinegar and stir fry for 15 seconds. Add the
cornflour mixture and stir until the sauce thickens.

Serve the fish in the cooking dish. Garnish it
with the vegetables and pour the sauce over it.

Sweet and Sour Whole Fish

Metric/Imperial

0.75–1 kg/1½–2 lb whole fish (trout, bream,
 carp, mullet, etc)
2 × 5 ml spoons/2 teaspoons salt
1.5 × 15 ml spoons/1½ tablespoons vegetable oil
3 × 15 ml spoons/3 tablespoons lard
2 small chilli peppers, finely sliced
6 spring onions
6 slices fresh ginger, shredded
1 red pepper, finely sliced
2–3 pieces bamboo shoot, chopped
1.5 × 15 ml spoons/1½ tablespoons sugar
1.5 × 15 ml spoons/1½ tablespoons tomato purée
3 × 15 ml spoons/3 tablespoons orange juice
3 × 15 ml spoons/3 tablespoons soy sauce
3 × 15 ml spoons/3 tablespoons wine vinegar
1 × 15 ml spoon/1 tablespoon cornflour, mixed
 with 5 × 15 ml spoons/5 tablespoons clear broth
 (page 82)

American

1½–3 lb whole fish (trout, bream,
 carp, mullet, etc)
2 teaspoons salt
1¼ tablespoons vegetable oil
3 tablespoons lard
2 small chili peppers, finely sliced
6 scallions
6 slices fresh ginger, shredded
1 red pepper, finely sliced
2–3 pieces bamboo shoot, chopped
1¼ tablespoons sugar
1½ tablespoons tomato paste
3 tablespoons orange juice
3 tablespoons soy sauce
1 tablespoon cornstarch, mixed
 with ⅓ cup clear broth
 (page 82)

Rub the fish, inside and out, with the salt and oil
and leave for 30 minutes. Arrange the fish in an oval
heatproof serving dish and place the dish in a
steamer. Steam vigorously for 15 minutes.

Heat the lard in a frying pan over moderate heat.
When the fat has melted add the chilli peppers and
stir and turn in the hot fat a few times. Cut the
spring onions into 5 cm/2 inch lengths and add all
the vegetables to the pan, with the sugar, tomato
purée (paste), orange juice, soy sauce and vinegar.
Stir fry for 15 seconds. Add the cornflour mixture
and stir until the sauce thickens. Pour the sauce
over the fish just before serving.

Right: Sweet and sour whole fish

Hot Pot

Chinese fire kettles, specially made for cooking this meal, are available from Chinese stores. They are heated with charcoal and look most impressive on the dining table. Alternatively you could use an adjustable spirit burner and a fondue pot. Either way you have a meal which is simple to prepare but most attractively presented.

Place small dishes of appetizers on the table and on a large platter arrange a selection of very thin slices of raw meat (fillet steak, lamb kidney, liver, veal kidney), whole prawns (shrimp), sliced scallops and fish fillets, and bite-sized pieces of cooked chicken. Allow a total of about 175 g/6 oz meat and fish per person. Serve a dish of fried or boiled rice, a crisp salad and a selection of sauces (below).

Fill the fire kettle with boiling chicken stock. Put this on the burner and keep the stock simmering. Add a 1 cm/½ inch slice of fresh ginger.

The guests serve themselves with rice and salad then select a piece of meat, fish or chicken with their chopsticks or forks and dip it into the simmering stock until it is cooked – about 1 or 2 minutes. They then dip the food into one of the sauces before eating it.

Soy and garlic sauce
Metric/Imperial
150 ml/¼ pint soy sauce
2 cloves garlic, crushed

American
⅔ cup soy sauce
2 cloves garlic, crushed

Blend the ingredients in a small saucepan, bring to the boil and simmer for 2 minutes.

Vinegar and ginger sauce
Metric/Imperial
1 × 15 ml spoon/1 tablespoon chopped fresh ginger
1 clove garlic, crushed
4 × 15 ml spoons/4 tablespoons vinegar
1 × 5 ml spoon/1 teaspoon sugar
pinch of monosodium glutamate
1 × 5 ml spoon/1 teaspoon tomato purée
salt
pepper

American
1 tablespoon chopped fresh ginger
1 clove garlic, crushed
⅓ cup vinegar
1 teaspoon sugar
pinch of monosodium glutamate
1 teaspoon tomato paste
salt
pepper

Mix all the ingredients together thoroughly.

Soy and ginger sauce
Metric/Imperial
150 ml/¼ pint soy sauce
2 × 5 ml spoons/2 teaspoons chopped fresh ginger
pinch of freshly ground black pepper

American
⅔ cup soy sauce
2 teaspoons chopped fresh ginger

Blend the ingredients together in a small saucepan, bring to the boil and simmer for 2 minutes.

Sweet and sour sauce
Metric/Imperial
2 × 15 ml spoons/2 tablespoons vinegar
2 × 15 ml spoons/2 tablespoons brown sugar
1 × 15 ml spoon/1 tablespoon cornflour
salt
pepper
150 ml/¼ pint chicken stock
1 × 5 ml/1 teaspoon tomato purée

American
2 tablespoons vinegar
2 tablespoons brown sugar
1 tablespoon cornstarch
salt
pepper
⅔ cup chicken stock
1 teaspoon tomato paste

Blend the vinegar, sugar and cornflour to a smooth paste, with salt and pepper to taste. Stir in the chicken stock and tomato purée (paste). Bring to boil, stirring constantly, simmer for 2 to 3 minutes.

Plum sauce
Metric/Imperial
6 × 15 ml spoons/6 tablespoons sieved plum jam
3 × 15 ml spoons/3 tablespoons chopped mango chutney
1 × 15 ml spoon/1 tablespoon vinegar
2 × 5 ml spoons/2 teaspoons sugar
salt
pepper

American
6 tablespoons sieved plum jam
3 tablespoons chopped mango chutney
1 tablespoon vinegar
2 teaspoons sugar
salt
pepper

Beat all the ingredients together, seasoning to taste.

Right: Hot pot

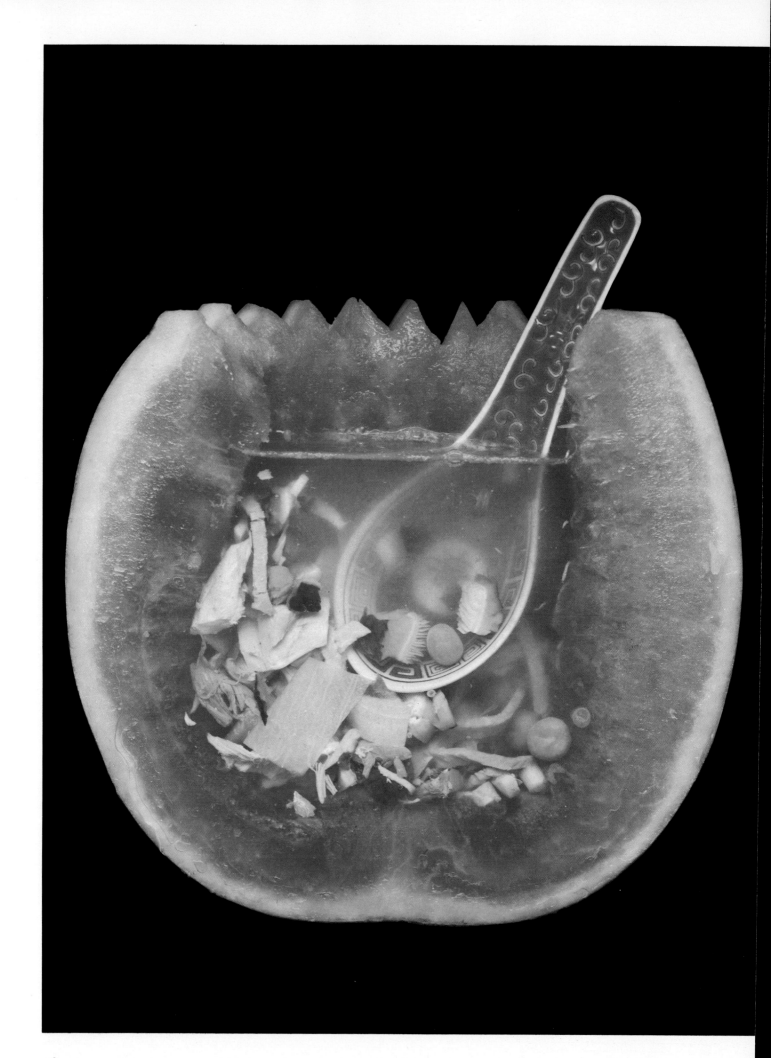

Soups

Chinese soups are served throughout the meal rather than as a starter. The majority are clear soups, based on a good broth with a variety of ingredients added to give flavour. The basic clear broth is also used in small quantities in other dishes – in a Chinese kitchen there would always be a big pot of broth available.

Crab and Vinegar Soup

Metric/Imperial
1 large cooked crab
vegetable oil
2 × 5 ml spoons/2 teaspoons salt
1 × 5 ml spoon/1 teaspoon chopped fresh ginger
2 tomatoes, sliced
1.2 litres/2 pints chicken stock
2 eggs, beaten
2 × 15 ml spoons/2 tablespoons sherry
2 × 15 ml spoons/2 tablespoons vinegar
2 × 15 ml spoons/2 tablespoons soy sauce
1 × 2.5 ml spoon/½ teaspoon monosodium glutamate

American
1 large cooked crab
vegetable oil
2 teaspoons salt
1 teaspoon chopped fresh ginger
2 tomatoes, sliced
5 cups chicken stock
2 eggs, beaten
2 tablespoons sherry
2 tablespoons vinegar
2 tablespoons soy sauce
½ teaspoon monosodium glutamate

Remove all the meat from the crab, discarding the sac and 'dead men's fingers'; chop the claw meat. Fry the meat in a little oil with half the salt and the ginger. Add the tomatoes and fry gently for 5 minutes. Add the chicken stock, bring to the boil and simmer for 15 minutes.

Add the eggs to the soup in a thin stream, so that they form ribbons. Add the remaining ingredients, stir well and serve immediately.

Left: Watermelon soup

Watermelon Soup

Metric/Imperial
25 g/1 oz dried mushrooms
100 g/4 oz bamboo shoots
600 ml/1 pint chicken stock
175 g/6 oz chicken, minced
175 g/6 oz pork, minced
100 g/4 oz lean ham, minced
1 × 2.5 ml spoon/½ teaspoon monosodium glutamate
100 g/4 oz shelled peas
1 × 2 kg/4 lb watermelon

American
1 oz dried mushrooms
2 cups bamboo shoots
2½ cups chicken stock
1½ cups chicken, ground
1½ cups pork, ground
1 cup lean ham, ground
½ teaspoon monosodium glutamate
¾ cup shelled peas
1 × 4 lb watermelon

Cut the mushrooms into small pieces and soak in boiling water for 1 hour. Cut the bamboo shoots into thin slices.

Bring the stock to the boil in a large saucepan. Add the chicken and pork and simmer for 10 minutes. Add the drained mushrooms, bamboo shoots and ham. Mix well and add the monosodium glutamate and peas.

Cut the top from the melon and scoop out the seeds and some of the pulp. Pour the soup into the melon and replace the top. Stand the melon in a basin and steam for about 1½ hours, until cooked.

The correct way to serve this soup is to place the melon on the table and scoop out soup and flesh, cutting the peel down as the level is lowered.

Mushroom Soup

Metric/Imperial
900 ml/1½ pints chicken stock
1 cm/½ inch slice fresh ginger
2 spring onions, sliced thinly
100 g/4 oz button mushrooms, sliced thinly
1 × 15 ml spoon/1 tablespoon sherry
salt
pepper

American
3¾ cups chicken stock
½ inch slice fresh ginger
2 scallions, sliced thinly
1 cup button mushrooms, sliced thinly
1 tablespoon sherry
salt
pepper

Put the stock in a saucepan with the ginger and spring onions. Bring to the boil and simmer, covered, for 20 minutes. Add the mushrooms and simmer for a further 10 minutes. Remove the ginger. Add the sherry and season to taste. Serve very hot.

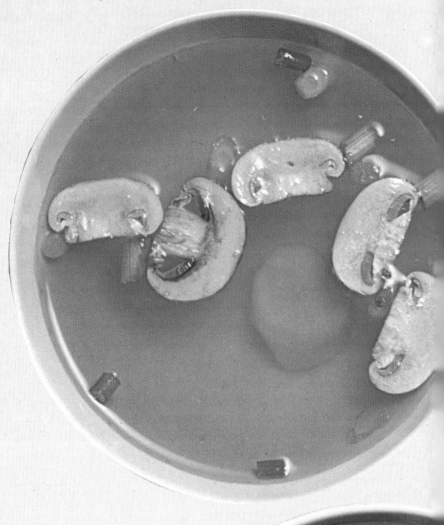

Egg Flower Soup Prawn and

Metric/Imperial
2 spring onions
900 ml/1½ pints chicken stock or clear broth
0.5 × 15 ml spoon/½ tablespoon dry sherry
pinch of monosodium glutamate
pinch of sugar
1 × 5 ml spoon/1 teaspoon soy sauce
175 g/6 oz peeled prawns
1 egg, well beaten
salt

American
2 scallions
3¾ cups chicken stock or clear broth
½ tablespoon dry sherry
pinch of monosodium glutamate
pinch of sugar
1 teaspoon soy sauce
1½ cups peeled shrimp
1 egg, well beaten
salt

Chop the spring onions finely and put them into a large saucepan with the stock. Bring to the boil and simmer, covered, for 10 minutes. Add the sherry, monosodium glutamate, sugar, soy sauce and prawns. Reheat gently until the prawns are heated through. Pour in the egg and stir until it separates into shreds. Add salt to taste. Serve immediately.

King prawns (Jumbo shrimps) should be deveined and cut in half.

Beef and Vegetable Soup

Metric/Imperial
100 g/4 oz beef topside
1 tomato
2 spring onions
6 water chestnuts
100 g/4 oz bamboo shoots
4 dried mushrooms
900 ml/1½ pints beef stock
pinch of monosodium glutamate
salt
pepper

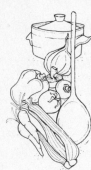

American
¼ lb beef topside
1 tomato
2 scallions
6 water chestnuts
2 cups bamboo shoots
4 dried mushrooms
3¾ cups beef stock
pinch of monosodium glutamate
salt
pepper

Cut the beef into thin strips across the grain of the meat. Skin the tomato and slice into four. Slice the spring onions, water chestnuts and bamboo shoots into thin strips. Soak the mushrooms in warm water for 20 minutes, rinse, squeeze dry and cut into thin strips, discarding the stalks.

Put the stock into a large saucepan and bring to the boil. Add the beef and simmer for 4 to 5 minutes. Add the vegetables and cook for 2 minutes. Add the monosodium glutamate and salt and pepper to taste.

Above left: Mushroom soup
Left: Prawn (shrimp) and egg flower soup
Above: Beef and vegetable soup

Abalone and Green Pea Soup

Metric/Imperial
4 dried mushrooms
1.2 litres/2 pints pork stock
100 g/4 oz lean pork
100 g/4 oz shelled peas
1 small can abalone
1 × 15 ml spoon/1 tablespoon soy sauce

American
4 dried mushrooms
5 cups pork stock
¼ lb lean pork
¾ cup shelled peas
1 small can abalone
1 tablespoon soy sauce

Slice the mushrooms and soak in boiling water for 30 minutes. Bring the stock to the boil. Shred the pork, add to the stock and simmer for 5 minutes. Add the peas and mushrooms and simmer for 5 minutes.

Drain the abalone, keeping the juice, and cut the abalone into small pieces. Add to the stock with the soy sauce, stir and serve immediately.

Egg Drop Soup

Metric/Imperial
2–3 spring onions
1 chicken stock cube
600 ml/1 pint hot clear broth
1 egg, beaten
1 × 5 ml spoon/1 teaspoon sesame oil
salt and pepper

American
2–3 scallions
1 chicken bouillon cube
2½ cups hot clear broth
1 egg, beaten
1 teaspoon sesame oil
salt and pepper

Cut the spring onions into rounds and divide between the serving bowls. Dissolve the stock cube in the broth and bring it to the boil. Remove from the heat and drip the egg in a narrow stream along the prongs of a fork into the broth, trailing it over the surface. Do not stir until the egg has set. Pour the soup into the bowls. Sprinkle with sesame oil, salt and pepper.

Clear Broth

Metric/Imperial
1 meaty chicken carcass
0.75 kg/1½ lb pork spare ribs
0.5 kg/1 lb bones from ham, beef or bacon
2 litres/3½ pints water
2 × 5 ml spoons/2 teaspoons salt

American
1 meaty chicken carcass
1½ lb pork spare ribs
1 lb bones from ham, beef or bacon
9 cups water
2 teaspoons salt

Put all the ingredients into a large, heavy-based saucepan. Bring to the boil and simmer gently for 1¾ hours, skimming any scum from the surface. Strain the broth and leave to cool. When it is cold, remove the fat from the surface and strain again.

Beef, Spinach and Tomato Soup

Metric/Imperial
225 g/8 oz stewing beef
100–175 g/4–6 oz spinach
4–5 medium tomatoes
2 spring onions
2 slices fresh ginger
600 ml/1 pint clear broth
½ chicken stock cube
salt
pepper

American
½ lb stewing beef
1–1½ cups spinach
4–5 medium tomatoes
2 scallions
2 slices fresh ginger
2½ cups clear broth
½ chicken bouillon cube
salt
pepper

Cut the beef into 12–15 pieces. Clean the spinach thoroughly, trim and chop. Cut the tomatoes into quarters and the spring onions into 1 cm/½ inch lengths. Chop the ginger.

Put the beef into a large, heavy based pan with the ginger and 600 ml/1 pint/2½ cups water. Bring to the boil and simmer gently for 1½ hours. Remove the ginger from the pan. Add the broth and crumbled stock cube and bring to the boil. Add the tomatoes, spinach and spring onions and return to the boil. Simmer gently for 3 to 4 minutes. Adjust the seasoning and serve in warmed bowls.

Right: Beef, spinach and tomato soup

Vegetables and snacks

The Chinese like their vegetables to be crisp and juicy. Vegetables are often used before they are fully grown, especially bean sprouts and spring onions, and they are very lightly cooked. Usually a minimum of liquid is added during cooking, the juice from the vegetable generally being sufficient.

Most meat dishes contain a high proportion of vegetables but a vegetable dish may also be served separately, like a salad.

Cold Sweet and Sour Radishes

Metric/Imperial
2 bunches small radishes
1 × 5 ml spoon/1 teaspoon salt
2 × 15 ml spoons/2 tablespoons soy sauce
1 × 15 ml spoon/1 tablespoon wine vinegar
1 × 15 ml spoon/1 tablespoon brown sugar
2 × 5 ml spoons/2 teaspoons sesame oil

American
2 bunches small radishes
1 teaspoon salt
2 tablespoons soy sauce
1 tablespoon wine vinegar
1 tablespoon brown sugar
2 teaspoons sesame oil

Wash, top and tail the radishes, and drain. Using a rolling pin, crush each radish, but do not break them completely – they must remain almost whole. Sprinkle with salt and leave for 5 minutes. Add the remaining ingredients, mix well and, when the sugar has dissolved, mix again. Serve chilled.

Left: A selection of vegetables, with noodles, that feature in Chinese cookery
Right: Cold asparagus (page 86), sweet and sour radishes, cucumber (page 86) and celery (page 88)

Cold Asparagus

Metric/Imperial

0.5 kg/1 lb asparagus
2 × 15 ml spoons/2 tablespoons soy sauce
1 × 5 ml spoon/1 teaspoon brown sugar
1 × 15 ml spoon/1 tablespoon olive oil
pinch of salt

American

1 lb asparagus
2 tablespoons soy sauce
1 teaspoon brown sugar
1 tablespoon olive oil
pinch of salt

Wash the asparagus and cut off the tough part of the stems. Put into a large pan, cover with boiling water and bring back to the boil. Simmer for 5 minutes. Drain. Rinse under cold running water until completely cold. Drain well.

Put the asparagus into a serving dish, add the soy sauce, sugar, oil and salt, mix well. Serve as a salad.

Cold Cucumber

Metric/Imperial

1 cucumber
1 × 2.5 ml spoon/½ teaspoon salt
1 × 15 ml spoon/1 tablespoon soy sauce
1 × 15 ml spoon/1 tablespoon wine vinegar
1 × 15 ml spoon/1 tablespoon caster sugar
2 × 5 ml spoons/2 teaspoons sesame oil

American

1 cucumber
½ teaspoon salt
1 tablespoon soy sauce
1 tablespoon wine vinegar
1 tablespoon superfine sugar
2 teaspoons sesame oil

Peel the cucumber and cut into small dice. Sprinkle with the remaining ingredients and leave for 5 minutes for the sugar to dissolve before serving.

Sweet and Sour Cabbage

Metric/Imperial

3 × 15 ml spoons/3 tablespoons oil or melted lard
1 large carrot, shredded or grated
3 tomatoes, chopped
1 × 15 ml spoon/1 tablespoon cornflour
150 ml/¼ pint stock or water
2 × 15 ml spoons/2 tablespoons soy sauce
1 × 5 ml spoon/1 teaspoon salt
1 × 15 ml spoon/1 tablespoon brown sugar
2 × 15 ml spoons/2 tablespoons wine vinegar
1 Chinese or Savoy cabbage
2 × 15 ml spoons/2 tablespoons sherry

American

3 tablespoons oil or melted lard
1 large carrot, shredded or grated
3 tomatoes, chopped
1 tablespoon cornstarch
⅔ cup stock or water
2 tablespoons soy sauce
1 tablespoon brown sugar
2 tablespoons wine vinegar
1 Chinese or Savoy cabbage
2 tablespoons sherry

Heat 1 × 15 ml spoon/1 tablespoon oil or lard in a pan and add the carrot and tomatoes. Fry for 2 to 3 minutes over a medium heat, stirring all the time. Mix the cornflour with a little of the stock or water, add the rest and the soy sauce, salt, brown sugar and vinegar. Add to the tomato mixture and bring to the boil, stirring all the time until thickened. Simmer gently whilst preparing the cabbage.

Clean and shred the cabbage and fry in the remaining oil or lard in another large pan, for 3 to 4 minutes, stirring constantly. Add the sherry, mix well and cook for 2 minutes. Pile the cabbage on to a dish and pour the sauce over. Serve immediately.

Right: Sweet and sour cabbage

Fried Rice with Mixed Vegetable Salad

Metric/Imperial

FRIED RICE:

4 × 15 ml spoons/4 tablespoons oil

2 × 15 ml spoons/2 tablespoons butter

1 large onion, sliced thinly

4 rashers streaky bacon, chopped

4 eggs, well beaten

100 g/4 oz shelled peas

0.5 kg/1 lb hot boiled rice

1.5 × 15 ml spoons/1½ tablespoons soy sauce

SALAD:

1 firm cos lettuce

100 g/4 oz bean sprouts, drained

2–3 tomatoes

2 sticks celery

½ bunch watercress

DRESSING:

2 spring onions

1 clove garlic, crushed

2 slices fresh ginger, grated

1.5 × 15 ml spoons/1½ tablespoons soy sauce

2 × 15 ml spoons/2 tablespoons wine vinegar

2 × 15 ml spoons/2 tablespoons clear broth
   (page 82)

1.5 × 5 ml spoons/1½ teaspoons sugar

1 × 15 ml spoon/1 tablespoon sesame oil

1 × 15 ml spoon/1 tablespoon olive oil

American

FRIED RICE:

⅓ cup oil

2 tablespoons butter

1 large onion, sliced thinly

4 slices fatty bacon, chopped

4 eggs, well beaten

½ cup shelled peas

3 cups boiled rice

1½ tablespoons soy sauce

SALAD:

1 firm romaine lettuce

¼ lb bean sprouts, drained

2–3 tomatoes

2 stalks celery

½ bunch watercress

DRESSING:

2 scallions

1 clove garlic, crushed

2 slices fresh ginger, grated

1½ tablespoons soy sauce

2 tablespoons wine vinegar

2 tablespoons clear broth
   (page 82)

1½ teaspoons sugar

1 tablespoon sesame oil

1 tablespoon olive oil

Heat the oil and butter in a large saucepan over moderate heat. When the fat has melted add the onion and bacon. Stir fry for 1½ minutes. Pour the beaten eggs into one half of the pan and add the peas to the other. Cook without stirring for 1 minute. Remove from the heat and leave until the eggs are just about to set. Stir the eggs into the other ingredients in the pan. Return the pan to the heat. Stir in the cooked rice and sprinkle with soy sauce. Keep hot.

Cut the salad vegetables into even-sized pieces. Cut the spring onions into thin rounds and combine with the garlic, ginger, soy sauce, vinegar, broth, sugar and oils until they are well blended. Put the salad vegetables in a bowl, add the dressing and toss well.

Arrange the fried rice on a heated serving plate and spoon the salad mixture on top.

Cold Celery

Metric/Imperial

1 head celery

pinch of salt

1 × 15 ml spoon/1 tablespoon soy sauce

1 × 5 ml spoon/1 teaspoon brown sugar

1 × 5 ml spoon/1 teaspoon sesame oil

American

1 bunch celery

pinch of salt

1 tablespoon soy sauce

1 teaspoon brown sugar

1 teaspoon sesame oil

Scrub the celery and cut into 2.5 cm/1 inch lengths. Put into a large pan, cover with cold water, bring to the boil, drain and immediately cover with cold water. Chill completely under cold running water. Drain. Add the salt, soy sauce, sugar and sesame oil. Mix well and serve chilled.

Right: Fried rice with mixed vegetable salad

Braised Mushrooms

Metric/Imperial
12 dried mushrooms
450 ml/¾ pint chicken stock
1 × 15 ml spoon/1 tablespoon soy sauce
2 spring onions, chopped
1 × 5 ml spoon/1 teaspoon very finely chopped fresh ginger
0.5 × 15ml spoon/½ tablespoon cornflour

American
12 dried mushrooms
2 cups chicken stock
1 tablespoon soy sauce
2 scallions
1 teaspoon very finely chopped fresh ginger
½ tablespoon cornstarch

Soak the mushrooms in warm water for 20 minutes, rinse and squeeze dry. Remove and discard the stalks. Pour the chicken stock into a saucepan, bring to the boil and add the mushrooms, soy sauce, spring onions and ginger. Cover and simmer for 1 to 1½ hours or until the mushrooms are very tender.

Put the mushrooms on to a serving plate and keep them warm. Mix the cornflour to a paste with a little cold water and add it to the liquid in the pan. Bring to the boil, stirring constantly, and simmer for 2 to 3 minutes. Pour the sauce over the mushrooms.

Cauliflower, Water Chestnuts and Mushrooms

Metric/Imperial
1 small cauliflower
8 water chestnuts
6 dried mushrooms
2 × 15 ml spoons/2 tablespoons vegetable oil
2 × 15 ml spoons/2 tablespoons cornflour
2 × 15 ml spoons/2 tablespoons soy sauce
2 × 15 ml spoons/2 tablespoons sherry
2 × 15 ml spoons/2 tablespoons stock

American
1 small cauliflower
8 water chestnuts
6 dried mushrooms
2 tablespoons vegetable oil
2 tablespoons cornstarch
2 tablespoons soy sauce
2 tablespoons sherry
2 tablespoons stock

Wash the cauliflower and break into florets, cover with boiling water and leave for 5 minutes. Drain. Cut the chestnuts into large pieces.

Cover the mushrooms with 300 ml/½ pint/1¼ cups boiling water, cover and leave for 30 minutes. Drain, but reserve the water. Cut the mushrooms into thin slices. Heat the oil and fry the mushrooms for 2 to 3 minutes over a fierce heat, stirring all the time. Add the chestnuts and cauliflower, mix well and cook for 2 minutes.

Mix the cornflour to a smooth paste with the remaining ingredients, add the mushroom water. Add to the pan and bring to the boil, stirring all the time until thickened. Cook for 2 to 3 minutes more then serve at once.

Braised Cabbage with Mushrooms

Metric/Imperial
0.5 kg/1 lb Chinese or Savoy cabbage
2 × 15 ml spoons/2 tablespoons peanut oil
1 green pepper
1 × 15 ml spoon/1 tablespoon soy sauce
1 × 5 ml spoon/1 teaspoon sugar
pinch of monosodium glutamate
100 g/4 oz button mushrooms
salt
pepper

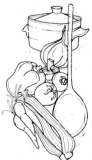

American
1 lb Chinese or Savoy cabbage
2 tablespoons peanut oil
1 green pepper
1 tablespoon soy sauce
1 teaspoon sugar
pinch of monosodium glutamate
1 cup button mushrooms
salt
pepper

Clean the cabbage and chop it roughly. Heat the oil in a saucepan, add the cabbage and fry for 2 to 3 minutes, stirring constantly. Cut the pepper into matchstick strips and add these to the pan with the soy sauce, sugar, monosodium glutamate and mushrooms. Season with salt and pepper. Add 4 × 15 ml spoons/4 tablespoons/⅓ cup water, cover the pan and cook for 5 to 7 minutes, shaking the pan occasionally. Put into a hot serving dish and serve immediately.

Right: Braised cabbage with mushrooms

Dim sum

The dishes in this section may be served either as side dishes within a main meal or as snacks. In general they are either quick to prepare, or can be stored for quick reheating.

Prawn Omelette

Metric/Imperial

4 eggs, beaten
50 g/2 oz peeled prawns
1 spring onion, finely chopped
pinch of salt
pinch of monosodium glutamate
175 ml/6 fl oz chicken stock
1 × 15 ml spoon/1 tablespoon oil
1 × 15 ml spoon/1 tablespoon soy sauce
1 × 15 ml spoon/1 tablespoon cornflour
1 × 5 ml spoon/1 teaspoon sugar

American

4 eggs, beaten
2 oz peeled shrimp
1 scallion, finely chopped
pinch of salt
pinch of monosodium glutamate
¾ cup chicken stock
1 tablespoon oil
1 tablespoon soy sauce
1 tablespoon cornstarch
1 teaspoon sugar

Mix the eggs with the prawns, onion, salt, monosodium glutamate and 2 × 15 ml spoons/2 tablespoons of the chicken stock. Heat the oil in a frying pan, pour in the mixture and fry until golden underneath, stirring occasionally with a fork. Continue cooking until just set. Cut into wedges and keep warm on a plate.

Put all the remaining ingredients in a saucepan, bring to the boil, stirring constantly, and simmer for 2 to 3 minutes. Pour the sauce over the omelette and serve immediately.

Spring Rolls

Metric/Imperial

225 g/8 oz lean pork, minced
100 g/4 oz peeled shrimps
1 × 15 ml spoon/1 tablespoon oil
225 g/8 oz bean sprouts
2 spring onions, chopped finely
1 × 15 ml spoon/1 tablespoon soy sauce
1 × 5 ml spoon/1 teaspoon salt
pinch of brown sugar
225 g/8 oz plain flour
600 ml/1 pint water
1 egg
oil for deep frying

American

½ lb lean pork, ground
¼ lb peeled shrimp
1 tablespoon oil
4 cups bean sprouts
2 scallions, chopped finely
1 tablespoon soy sauce
1 teaspoon salt
pinch of brown sugar
2 cups all-purpose flour
2½ cups water
1 egg
oil for deep frying

Mix the pork and shrimps together and fry in oil for 2 minutes. Drain the bean sprouts and add with the spring onions to the pork. Mix well and cook for 2 minutes. Stir in the soy sauce, salt and sugar.

Mix the flour, water and egg to a smooth batter. Using a heavy based frying pan, lightly oiled, make 16 very thin pancakes, cooked on one side only. Place some of the mixture on each one; fold the edge nearest you to the centre, fold both sides in to the centre, then roll up, sealing the last edge with a little water. Make all the rolls like this then fry in deep hot oil for about 15 minutes, turning the rolls during cooking to ensure even browning. Drain well and serve very hot.

Right: Prawn (shrimp) chop suey (page 52), sweet and sour prawns (shrimp) (page 56) and prawn (shrimp) omelette

Fried Hun T'un

Metric/Imperial

0.5 kg/1 lb hun t'un paste
0.5 kg/1 lb streaky pork, minced
2 × 15 ml spoons/2 tablespoons soy sauce
1 × 5 ml spoon/1 teaspoon brown sugar
1 × 5 ml spoon/1 teaspoon salt
350 g/12 oz frozen leaf spinach
oil for deep frying

American

1 lb hun t'un paste
1 lb fatty pork, ground
2 tablespoons soy sauce
1 teaspoon brown sugar
1 teaspoon salt
¾ lb frozen leaf spinach
oil for deep frying

Cut out 5 cm/2 inch rounds from the paste. Mix the pork with the soy sauce, sugar and salt and mix well. Leave for 10 minutes. Defrost the spinach and squeeze in a clean, dry cloth to remove excess moisture. Add the pork and mix well.

Put a little of the spinach mixture in the centre of each round of paste, damp the edges and press together to seal. Drop the hun t'un into hot deep oil and fry for about 5 minutes, turning them during cooking to brown them evenly. Drain and serve hot.

Boiled Pastry Balls

Metric/Imperial

225 g/8 oz lean pork, minced
2 × 15 ml spoons/2 tablespoons soy sauce
1 × 5 ml spoon/1 teaspoon sherry
1 spring onion, chopped finely
few drops sesame oil
1 × 15 ml spoon/1 tablespoon cornflour
pinch of salt
225 g/8 oz rice flour
about 150 ml/¼ pint hot water

American

½ lb lean pork, ground
2 tablespoons soy sauce
1 teaspoon sherry
1 scallion, chopped finely
few drops sesame oil
1 tablespoon cornstarch
pinch of salt
2 cups rice flour
about ⅔ cup hot water

Mix the pork with the soy sauce and sherry. Add the spring onion, sesame oil, cornflour and salt and beat until well blended.

Mix the rice flour and hot water together to make

a soft dough, adding more water if necessary. Divide the dough into 24 pieces and shape each into a ball. Make a hole in the centre of each ball and press some of the pork filling into the middle. Shape the dough around the filling and pinch the edges together. Drop the balls into a large pan of salted boiling water, allow it to come back to the boil and boil for 5 minutes. Add 300 ml/½ pint/1¼ cups cold water to the pan, bring back to the boil and boil for another 3 minutes.

Drain the balls and serve four or more to each person with a little of the boiling water. Use a spoon to eat them, in order to catch the juices from the centre as the first bite is taken.

Pasties

Metric/Imperial

350 g/12 oz minced beef
4 × 15 ml spoons/4 tablespoons oil
6 spring onions
100 g/4 oz white cabbage heart
1 × 15 ml spoon/1 tablespoon soy sauce
1 × 5 ml spoon/1 teaspoon salt
350 g/12 oz plain flour
1 egg
150 ml/¼ pint hot stock or water

American

¾ lb ground beef
¼ cup oil
6 scallions
¼ lb white cabbage heart
1 tablespoon soy sauce
1 teaspoon salt
3 cups all-purpose flour
1 egg
⅔ cup hot stock or water

Fry the beef in half the oil for 10 minutes. Chop the spring onions and cabbage finely, add to the pan and cook for 2 to 3 minutes. Add the soy sauce and salt, mix well and leave until cold.

Mix the flour and egg together with enough cold water to make a soft dough. Turn on to a floured surface and knead lightly. Roll out the dough very thinly and cut into 7.5 cm/3 inch rounds. Place a little of the beef mixture in the centre of each round; damp the edges with water and press together to seal.

Fry the pasties in the remaining oil for 3 minutes, turning them once. Add the hot stock or water, cover the pan and simmer for 5 minutes.

Right: Steamed rolls (page 96), fried hun t'un, pasties and boiled pastry balls

Steamed Rolls

Metric/Imperial
15 g/½ oz fresh yeast
600 ml/1 pint warm water
0.75 kg/1½ lb plain flour
salt
oil

American
½ cake compressed yeast
2½ cups warm water
6 cups all-purpose flour
salt
oil

Blend the yeast with the water, add the liquid to the flour and knead it in until the dough is smooth and elastic; this takes about 5 minutes. Put into a clean bowl and leave, covered, in a warm place for about 1½ hours or until the dough has doubled its original size.

Turn it on to a floured board and knead lightly. Divide the dough into two pieces and roll out each to an oblong about 38 cm/15 inches long and 10 cm/4 inches wide. Sprinkle with salt and oil. Roll each piece up from the long side to make two sausage shapes. Cut into short lengths and leave in a warm place for about 10 minutes. Steam for 20 minutes.

The rolls can be stored in a cold place and reheated without loss of flavour or texture.

Liang-far Eggs

Metric/Imperial
2 dried mushrooms
100 g/4 oz Chinese cabbage or spinach
4 sticks celery
150 g/5 oz bamboo shoots
2 × 5 ml spoons/2 teaspoons soy sauce
1 × 15 ml spoon/1 tablespoon dry sherry
1 × 2.5 ml spoon/½ teaspoon sugar
150 ml/¼ pint chicken stock
1 × 15 ml spoon/1 tablespoon cornflour
pinch of monosodium glutamate
oil for frying
1 clove garlic, crushed
1 × 2.5 ml spoon/½ teaspoon salt
6 eggs
lettuce for serving

American
2 dried mushrooms
¼ lb Chinese cabbage or spinach
4 stalks celery
5 oz bamboo shoots
2 teaspoons soy sauce
1 tablespoon dry sherry
½ teaspoon sugar
⅔ cup chicken stock
1 tablespoon cornstarch
pinch of monosodium glutamate
oil for frying
1 clove garlic, crushed
½ teaspoon salt
6 eggs
lettuce for serving

Soak the mushrooms in warm water for 20 minutes, rinse, squeeze dry and slice thinly, discarding the stalks. Shred the cabbage finely. Cut the celery diagonally. Cut the bamboo shoots into thin strips. Mix together the soy sauce, sherry, sugar, stock, cornflour and monosodium glutamate. Heat 1 × 15 ml spoon/1 tablespoon oil in a saucepan with the garlic and salt. Add the prepared vegetables and fry, stirring, for 2 to 3 minutes. Stir the cornflour mixture and add it to the pan. Bring to the boil, stirring, and simmer for 2 to 3 minutes. Keep hot.

Heat about 2.5 cm/1 inch oil in a small frying pan. Fry the eggs. Arrange the lettuce on a serving dish, put the eggs on top and pour the sauce over.

Right: Liang-far eggs

Sweet dishes

The Chinese do not often serve a separate sweet dish. More often sweet ingredients are included within a savoury dish to add subtlety to the flavour. There are a few traditional sweet dishes, however, and these may be served at the end of a meal, as a dessert.

Almond Lake with Mandarin Oranges

Metric/Imperial
600 ml/1 pint milk
100 g/4 oz granulated sugar
1 × 5 ml spoon/1 teaspoon almond essence
50 g/2 oz ground rice
1 × 300 g/11 oz can mandarin oranges
25 g/1 oz flaked, brown almonds

American
2½ cups milk
½ cup sugar
1 teaspoon almond extract
⅓ cup ground rice
1 × 11 oz can mandarin oranges
¼ cup flaked, toasted almonds

Put the milk, sugar, almond essence and rice in a small saucepan. Bring to the boil, stirring constantly, and simmer for 5 minutes. Pour into a dish, cover and cool.

Drain the mandarin oranges. Spoon the rice into individual dishes. Place the oranges on top of the rice and scatter the almonds over.

Almond Cream with Chow Chow

Metric/Imperial
1 × 0.5 kg/16 oz can chow chow or mixed fruit salad
600 ml/1 pint water
25 g/1 oz gelatine
450 ml/¾ pint milk
sugar to taste
1 × 5 ml spoon/1 teaspoon almond essence

American
1 × 1 lb can chow chow or mixed fruit salad
2½ cups water
4 envelopes gelatin
2 cups milk
sugar to taste
1 teaspoon almond extract

Chop the larger pieces of chow chow in half or drain the fruit salad. Put 4 × 15 ml spoons/4 tablespoons/¼ cup water in a small bowl and stand it in a saucepan of hot water. Shower the gelatine into the bowl and heat, stirring, until dissolved.

Heat the remaining water with the milk, sugar and almond essence, stirring until the sugar has dissolved. Stir in the gelatine. Pour into a shallow, lightly oiled cake tin and chill until set.

Cut the almond cream into triangular bite-sized pieces. Put these in a serving bowl with the fruit and mix very gently. Serve chilled.

Left: Almond cream with chow chow

Caramel Apples

Metric/Imperial
6 apples
40 g/1½ oz plain flour
15 g/½ oz cornflour
2 egg whites
oil for deep frying
100 g/4 oz granulated sugar
1 × 15 ml spoon/1 tablespoon oil
1 × 15 ml spoon/1 tablespoon sesame seeds

American
6 apples
6 tablespoons all-purpose flour
2 tablespoons cornstarch
2 egg whites
oil for deep frying
½ cup sugar
1 tablespoon oil
1 tablespoon sesame seeds

Peel, core and quarter the apples. Dust them lightly with some of the flour. Sift the remaining flour with the cornflour into a bowl. Add the egg whites and mix to a paste. Add the apple quarters and stir to coat in paste. Deep fry in hot oil until golden. Drain well on absorbent kitchen paper.

Put the sugar in a small saucepan with 2 × 15 ml spoons/2 tablespoons water. Heat, stirring, until the sugar has dissolved. Add the oil and continue heating slowly until the sugar has caramelized and is a light golden brown. Stir in the apple and sesame seeds. Serve immediately in individual serving dishes that have been very lightly oiled. Put a bowl of cold water on the table so that each piece of apple can be dipped in it before eating, for the caramel to harden.

Fried Sweet Potato

Metric/Imperial
0.5 kg/1 lb sweet potatoes
oil for shallow frying
6 × 15 ml spoons/6 tablespoons golden syrup

American
1 lb sweet potatoes
oil for shallow frying
6 tablespoons light corn syrup

Thickly peel the potatoes and cut into sticks about 1 cm/½ inch wide and 5–7.5 cm/2–3 inches long. Dry the sticks on a clean towel and fry them in the oil for about 4 minutes or until golden brown and crisp. Drain and pile on a large dish. Heat the syrup and pour it over the potatoes.

If they are obtainable, use small sweet potatoes as they are easier to handle.

Chilled Melon Bowl

Metric/Imperial
1 large melon or watermelon
1 small can lychees in syrup
4–5 × 15 ml spoons/4–5 tablespoons preserved
    ginger
any mixture of fresh and canned fruit

American
1 large melon or watermelon
1 small can lychees in syrup
¼–⅓ cup preserved ginger
any mixture of fresh and canned
    fruit

Slice 5 cm/2 inches from the top of the melon. Remove the seeds and scoop out the flesh carefully, in large pieces. Cut into even sized pieces. Mix the melon pieces with the other fruits and fill the cavity of the melon with the mixture. Chill for 2 to 3 hours.

Remove the melon from the refrigerator and top with a piece (or several pieces) of ice. Serve the fruit salad from the melon shell.

Gingered Fruit

Metric/Imperial
1 × 425 g/15 oz can pineapple pieces
1 × 300 g/11 oz can lychees
1 × 15 ml spoon/1 tablespoon chopped glacé
    cherries
2 × 15 ml spoons/2 tablespoons chopped
    crystallized ginger
25 g/1 oz toasted flaked almonds

American
1 × 15 oz can pineapple pieces
1 × 11 oz can lychees
1 tablespoon chopped candied
    cherries
2 tablespoons chopped preserved
    ginger
¼ cup toasted flaked almonds

Drain the syrup from the canned fruits. Lightly mix the pineapple, lychees, cherries and ginger in a serving bowl. Chill well. Sprinkle the almonds on top and serve immediately.

Right: Chilled melon bowl

Steamed Honeyed Pears

Metric/Imperial

4 medium or large pears
4 × 15 ml spoons/4 tablespoons sugar
4 × 15 ml spoons/4 tablespoons clear honey
2 × 15 ml spoons/2 tablespoons Chinese 'rose dew', cherry brandy or crème de menthe

American

4 medium or large pears
¼ cup sugar
⅓ cup clear honey
2 tablespoons Chinese 'rose dew', cherry brandy or crème de menthe

Peel the pears, leaving on the stem and a little of the surrounding skin for ease of handling. Stand them in a saucepan and just cover with water. Bring to the boil over low heat and simmer for 30 minutes. Pour off half the water, sprinkle the pears with the sugar and simmer for a further 10 minutes. Remove the pears from the pan and chill in the refrigerator for 2 hours.

Meanwhile pour off a further half of the water in the pan. Add the honey and liqueur to what is left and stir until well blended. Chill.

Serve the pears in individual dishes, with the honey sauce poured over.

Eight Treasures Rice

Metric/Imperial

175 g/6 oz short grain rice
100 g/4 oz brown sugar
50 g/2 oz dates
50 g/2 oz blanched almonds
50 g/2 oz walnuts
50 g/2 oz glacé cherries
50 g/2 oz mixed peel
50 g/2 oz raisins
50 g/2 oz glacé pineapple, appricots or figs as available

American

¾ cup short grain rice
⅔ cup brown sugar
½ cup dates
½ cup blanched almonds
½ cup walnuts
⅓ cup candied cherries
½ cup candied peel
½ cup raisins
⅓ cup candied pineapple, apricots or figs as available

Cook the rice in boiling water for about 15 minutes or until tender. Drain and stir in the sugar. Arrange a layer of fruit and nuts, in a pattern, in the base of an oiled bowl (capacity 900 ml–1.2 litres/1½–2 pints/3¾–5 cups), this will be seen as decoration when the dessert is unmoulded. Add a layer of rice, then a layer of mixed nuts and fruit. Continue layering until all the ingredients have been used, finishing with a layer of rice.

Press down very firmly and cover with greased foil. Put the bowl in a steamer and steam for 30 to 40 minutes. Unmould on to a flat plate and serve hot.

Below: Steamed honeyed pears
Right: Eight treasures rice

Index

ACKNOWLEDGEMENTS

The publishers would like to thank the following organisations and individuals for their kind permission to reproduce the photographs in this book:

American Rice Council 42, 60; Bryce Attwell 21, 87; Barry Bullough 12, 59, 62, 65, 67, 69, 77, 80–81, 91, 97, 98, 103; Conway Picture Library 11; Gales Honey 23, 35; Melvin Grey 6, 9, 15, 22, 29, 37, 39, 41, 70, 71, 73, 75, 83, 89, 101, 102; Paul Kemp 16–17, 26–27, 45, 53, 61, 78; John Lee 18, 40, 44, 47, 55, 84, 85; Neil Lorriner 7, 25, 30, 48, 49, 51; Syndication International 10, 24; Young's Seafoods 93; John West 63.